£6.56

3/97

UNIVERSITY OF WOLVERHAMPTON

LR/LEND/001

Wolverhampton Learning Centre
University of Wolverhampton
St Peter's Square
Wolverhampton WV1 1RH
Wolverhampton (01902) 322305

Telephone Renewals: 01902 321333
**This item may be recalled at any time. Keeping it after it has
been recalled or beyond the date stamped may result in a fine.**
See tariff of fines displayed at the counter.

1 8 NOV 1999	1 1 DEC 2007
2 -	
	2 0 FEB 2007 - 9 NOV 2010 196
1 2 APR 2000	
	2 0 APR 2007 3 1 JAN 2011
1 8 MAY 2000	
0 5 MAR 2001	
	1 5 MAY 2007
snown above	L I

SITE PRACTICE SERIES

General editors: Harold Lansdell, FCIOB, FCIArb, and
  Win Lansdell, BA

Timber-frame housing – *Jim Burchell*
Security on site – *Len Earnshaw*
Site safety – *Jim Laney*
Site engineering – *Roy Murphy*
Glazing – *Stanley Thompson*
Steel reinforcement – *Tony Trevorrow*

Books to be published in the Series
Making and placing concrete – *Edwin Martin Baker*
Site carpentry and joinery – *Keith Farmer*
Industrial relations on site – *Tom Gallagher*
Careers in the building industry – *Chris and Lynne March*
Fixings, fasteners and adhesives – *Paul Marsh*
Exercises in brickwork and blockwork – *Arthur Webster*

Timber-frame housing

JIM BURCHELL

Construction Press

LONDON AND NEW YORK

Construction Press
an imprint of:
Longman Group Limited
Longman House, Burnt Mill, Harlow
Essex CM20 2JE, England
Associated companies throughout the world

Published in the United States of America
by Longman Inc., New York

First published 1984

British Library Cataloguing in Publication Data
Burchell, Jim
   Timber-frame housing. — (Site practice series)
   I. Wooden-frame houses — Design and construction
   I. Title   II. Series
   694   TH4818.W6

   ISBN 0-86095-713-6

Library of Congress Cataloging in Publication Data
Burchell, Jim.
   Timber-frame housing.

   (Site practice series)
   Bibliography: p.
   Includes index.
   1. Wooden-frame houses — Great Britain.   I. Title.
II. Series.
TH4818.W6B87   1984   690'.837   83-7556
ISBN 0-86095-713-6

Set in 10/12pt Linotron 202 Bembo
Printed in Hong Kong by
Astros Printing Ltd

Contents

The views and comments expressed in this book are my own and not necessarily those of FrameForm Ltd of which I am a director.

J. BURCHELL

Preface

The use of timber-frame construction for house building in the UK has increased steadily over the past few years and is still increasing. At the time of writing this preface, November 1982, current statistics indicate that 27 per cent of all housing being built in the UK is was of timber-frame construction. This radical change in construction techniques has meant that, in the majority of cases, the building operatives on site have been faced with a method of building completely foreign to them and, indeed, a method which necessitates a completely different approach from everything their training and experience has taught them in connection with masonry construction.

During the past decade, many study tours, seminars, lecture tours, film shows etc. have been promoted by such organizations as the Timber Research and Development Association, Council of Forest Industries of British Columbia and the British Woodworking Federation, to emphasize the advantages of timber-frame construction. These have, in the main, been directed towards middle and top management, and have proved most successful in convincing management to make the change from masonry to timber frame. For a long time, I have considered, however, that not enough was being done to explain the new form of construction to the man on site and, for this reason, when my friends of many years' standing, Harold and Win Lansdell, approached me about writing this book, I readily agreed.

I might also add that, because of the increase in the use of timber-frame housing, regulations laid down in the Building Regulations, NHBC regulations, Codes of Practice and British Standard Specifications are continually changing and, while I have endeavoured to avoid questions of design and compliance with regulations, I have, at times, not been able to avoid such things in order to illustrate a point. These references were as up to date as I could keep them when writing during the summer of 1982.

Acknowledgements

We are grateful to the following for permission to reproduce copyright material:

British Gypsum Ltd for Figs 9.1 and 9.2; Cape Insulation Ltd for Figs 7.2, 7.3 and 7.4; Council of Forest Industries of British Columbia for Figs 6.1, 6.2 and 6.3; French Kier Construction Ltd for Fig. 3.1; Gee Walker & Slater Ltd for Figs 1.2, 2.1, 2.2, 4.3, 4.4, 4.5, 4.6, 4.7, 4.8 and 12.1; Kwikform Ltd for Fig. 3.2; Norman Ltd, Jersey for Figs 8.4, 8.5, 8.6 and 8.7; Norman Piette Ltd, Guernsey, for Figs 8.2, 8.3, 8.8, 11.2, 11.3 and 11.4; Potton Homes Ltd for Fig. 1.3; and Ian Russell for Figs 1.4 and 1.5.

1

Brief history and description of timber-frame construction

Historical introduction

Some of the oldest buildings still existing in the UK today are timber-framed (see Fig. 1.1). However, the current methods of constructing timber-frame housing by using structural framing timbers of dressed softwood started to become popular when the Building Regulations were amended in April 1965, allowing this form of construction without the need for waivers that had hitherto been necessary. The change in the Building Regulations followed a Canadian government-sponsored visit to Canada by a UK party, which included Sir Donald Gibson, who was then Director-General of Research and Development, Ministry of Public Buildings and Works, responsible for the Building Regulations. This change,

Fig. 1.1 Ancient timber frame still standing in Suffolk.

together with the government's call for more houses to be built using less labour, and the sales drive of the Canadians, Swedes and Finns, all helped to make timber-frame housing the acceptable method of construction it is today. The Canadians probably had the greatest influence and the basic principles of timber-frame housing in the UK are based on what is considered traditional house building in Canada.

It is interesting to note that there is a school of thought believing that the early emigrants to Canada from the UK arrived with their knowledge of and skills in the timber-frame housing then being used in the UK, i.e. large-section timbers connected by a complicated jointing technique and held together by wooden pegs or pellets inserted in holes. The subsequent advent of machinery to produce small-section wrought timbers, the invention of the nail and the availability of high-quality softwood, enabled those early skills to be converted to what the Canadians now call their traditional method of building houses and which we are now copying in this country.

Brief description of timber-frame construction

In a timber-frame house, all loadbearing and non-loadbearing elements above the concrete slab, i.e. walls, floors and roofs, are engineered and constructed in timber and plywood. Any form of cladding and roof covering may be used. The claddings are never structural, but purely decorative and an aid to protecting the timber frame from the elements.

Advantages

The main advantages of timber-frame construction are:

1 Speed of erection.
2 Higher degree of thermal insulation more easily attainable than with traditional construction.
3 Dry construction, needing no time for drying-out on completion.
4 Economy in construction.
5 Less wastage of materials
6 Higher standard of finish attainable.
7 Less maintenance.

These advantages are described in greater detail in Chapter 12.

Contractors with experience of timber-frame construction will not necessarily put these advantages in the order shown above but there is little doubt that they will agree that most, if not all, the advantages exist, hence the great increase in the number of timber-frame houses built in the UK over the past few years.

Types of timber-frame construction

The four main forms of timber-frame construction for housing are platform frame, balloon frame, post and beam, and volumetric.

Platform-frame construction (see Fig. 1.2)

This form of construction is the most commonly used in Canada, the USA and the UK. It can best be described as structural timber-stud panels replacing the internal partitions and inner leaf of external walls of traditional construction. All the timber panels are storey-height and the ground-floor panels support the floor joists. These are usually covered with 16 mm tongued-and-grooved plywood, extending over the whole area of the house formed by the ground-floor frame. Thus, a platform is formed on which to erect the next floor in similar manner. All upper wall panels, both external and internal, are supported on the plywood floor deck over the floor joists. One-, two- and three-storey dwellings may be constructed by this method under current Building Regulations in the UK.

The advantages of platform frame include:

(a) no mechanical equipment is needed to load, unload and erect where prefabricated small-panel timber frames are used, as is normal in the UK;

(b) storey-height studs are readily and economically available;

(c) it can be erected without scaffolding;

(d) it provides complete freedom of layout and fenestration to the designer;

(e) as timber shrinks mostly in its width, not in its length, it follows that, with platform-frame construction, most shrinkage takes place in the joist zone, where it has little effect on finishes.

Balloon-frame construction

This form of construction is where the external timber frames extend from sole-plate level to eaves. The external panels having

Fig. 1.2 FrameForm platform-frame houses under construction. Note that the ground-floor components are erected well ahead of first-floor components which, in turn, are well ahead of roof trusses.

Fig. 1.3 Modern post-and-beam cottage from the Heritage range by Potton Homes Ltd.

been erected, the roof trusses are placed in position and the floor joists inserted on a waist-band let into the studs of the external panels. Internal panels are put up after the roof is in position. Balloon frame is seldom used today because of the high cost and short supply of the long lengths of timber required; the difficulty in transporting and handling such large panels in factories and on site; the need for mechanical equipment on site; and the differential movement between panels sitting on joists and the external wall components.

Post-and-beam construction

This is a form of construction where large-section timber beams are supported on large-section timber posts, thus forming a structural grid frame similar in concept to a structural steel frame for large buildings.

The external infill panels and internal partition panels are usually identical to those used in platform-frame construction, in order to achieve the necessary standards of acoustic and thermal insulation and also to provide the necessary standards of wind and impact resistance. It will be seen, therefore, that the posts and beams become somewhat superfluous, because the infill and partition panels are normally capable of supporting the structural loads. However, in one-off houses, fine 'olde worlde' designs can be produced with this method of construction, with exposed posts and beams as shown in Fig. 1.3. Some economy in design is also being achieved by cantilevering beams over the posts and so reducing the number of posts required, illustrated in Fig. 1.4

Volumetric housing units

What is now generally referred to as volumetric housing is the practice of off-site manufacture of completely finished timber-frame storey-height boxes which are then joined together on site to form a housing unit (see Fig. 1.5).

While claddings and external colours can be varied on a site, the repetitive appearance of the units is not always acceptable to architects and planners.

Manufacturers of volumetric units claim great savings in costs as the major part of the building operations is undertaken in controlled factory conditions but set against this must be the cost of cranage required in the factory and on the site, transport of large loads with size limitations due to transport regulations and the fact that builder/developers look for their building profit as well

6

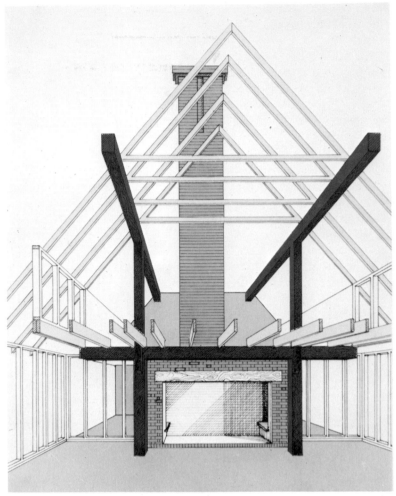

Fig. 1.4 Post-and-beam construction showing cantilevered beams and timber-frame panels as used in the Heritage range.

as their developer's profit. The completed boxes are sold to the builder/developer with the manufacturer's profit included but, when the price of the house for sale is calculated, the builder/developer will want his profit on the total cost to him of the house and land. However, volumetric housing is gaining in popularity at the moment, probably partly due to the demand for small houses for the first-time buyer.

For the reasons stated above, the remainder of this book refers only to platform-frame construction.

7

Fig. 1.5 Volumetric unit by Potton Timber Engineering Co. Ltd. being off-loaded and placed in position on site.

Details of timber normally used

The design of all timber-frame housing is engineered and must, therefore, be precise. In the UK, the structural design must comply with Code of Practice BSCP 112: Part 2: 1971 in order to obtain approval under the Building Regulations. Selection of the correct timber to be used is of paramount importance. The designer must know the relevant strength properties of the timber he specifies. Besides selecting the species, or group of species with like properties, he must be able to identify the strong and the weak pieces within the species. Unlike other structural materials, which can be manufactured to comply with a specific strength property, timber, being of organic origin, must be accepted as covering a wide range of strength properties. The designer must, therefore, select the species, or group of species with like properties, the overall strength characteristics of which are known and recorded as a result of extensive testing. Within the species, further classification is carried out by stress grading (referred to in Canada as stress rating), in order to sort the stronger pieces from the weaker.

Most local authorities in the UK demand structural calculations for study before granting approval under the Building Regulations. The designer has, therefore, to specify species, grade, size and moisture content of the timber to be used and it is essential to ensure that the specification used in the preparation of the approved calculations is identical in all respects to that used on site. A fact often overlooked here is that the size of timber will vary according to its moisture content, as timber swells when wet and shrinks when drying out. It is, therefore, imperative always to combine size with moisture content.

Structural framing members

The Canadians produce timber specifically for timber-frame housing. It is known as Canadian Lumber Specification (C.L.S.). Because the market for Canadian timber is still predominantly in those countries still using Imperial dimensions for timber – USA etc. – C.L.S. is marketed in nominal Imperial dimensions – 2 × 3 in, 2 × 4 in, 2 × 6 in, 2 × 8 in, 2 × 10 in and 2 × 12 in. The lengths increase by 2 ft increments from 8 ft. C.L.S. is stress graded, planed on all four sides, with all arrises rounded, and normally kiln-dried (see Fig. 1.6). The exception is with Hem/Fir (hemlock fir) C.L.S. which is not kiln-dried but machined and shipped green. For this reason, S.P.F. (spruce, pine, fir) C.L.S. is generally preferred to Hem/Fir for framing members, as described more fully later in this chapter. Actual metric sizes of nominal C.L.S. timbers are as follows;

nominal (in)	actual (mm)
2 × 3	38 × 64
2 × 4	38 × 89
2 × 6	38 × 140
2 × 8	38 × 184
2 × 10	38 × 235
2 × 12	38 × 286

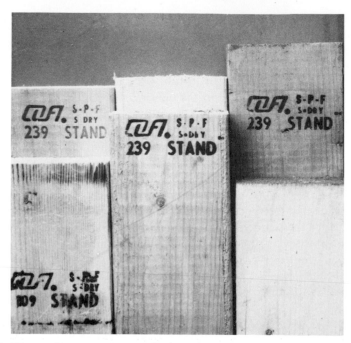

Fig. 1.6 Pieces of 38 × 89 mm standard-grade C.L.S. The grade stamps also show registered number of COFI Mill that produced the C.L.S., species (in this case S.P.F. for Spruce, Pine, Fir) and that it was kiln-dried before dressing (dry).

C.L.S. dimensions are always quoted at 19 per cent moisture content. However, C.L.S. will not always be specified. Sometimes, depending upon economics and availability, European timber will be specified to a specific size and moisture content. This could be the same as for C.L.S. or could differ, especially with joists. For example, a common size of joist section used in the UK is 44 × 194 mm at 19 per cent moisture content. This is often supplied in Canadian Spruce No. 1 and No. 2 grades, regularized in this country out of 47 × 200 mm sawn material. As sawn material is not kiln-dried before shipping, when it arrives in the UK, it should be stored under cover and stacked so as to allow air circulation inside the stack to reduce the moisture content to 20 per cent before regularizing down. This method of stacking is known as 'sticking' or 'in stick'. Regularizing, as opposed to dressed four sides, is a more hit-and-miss method of taking off less material, sometimes leaving one sawn edge and one sawn face and, sometimes, two sawn faces. The designer must always specify the species, grade, size and moisture content of timber which his design and calculations demand. In Canada, the National Lumber Grades Authority (NLGA) have standards of grading that are acceptable under the Building Regulations in the UK. Under their Light Framing Classification covering studs, plates etc. (38 × 89 mm, i.e. ex 2 × 4 in), there are two main grades – Construction and Standard. Their Structural Light Framing Classification also covers the same-size material but is graded No. 1 and No. 2. No. 1 is generally better than Construction and No. 2 is better than Standard but inferior to Construction. It is essential to understand this, as a specification may call for a particular grade or better. Under the NLGA Structural Joists and Planks classification covering joist and lintel material generally, there are two main grades – No. 1 and No. 2.

When timber arrives in the UK ungraded, before it can be used in an engineered timber frame, it has to be visually or mechanically graded in accordance with BS 4978. Visual stress grading is carried out either by quantifying the effect of knots, slope of grain etc. (collectively known as defects) and producing a numerical coded grade classification representing 40, 50, 65, or 75 per cent of the strength of clear timber, or by assessing the knot area ratio resulting in two grades – SS (Select Structural) and GS (General Structural). When the grading is carried out mechanically, the codes are prefixed by the letter M.

It has been proposed to confine visual grading to SS and GS grades only, which will mean that, to grade timber to the 40, 50, 65 and 75 grades, grading machines will have to be used.

The Building Research Establishment have published an Information Paper (IP 4/82) on the subject of stress grading.

As a guide only, the following lists show the various grades in order – best grade first in each case.

Studs and plates (38 × 89 mm)

S.P.F. No. 1	(Canadian NLGA)
S.P.F. Construction	(Canadian NLGA)
S.P.F. No. 2	(Canadian NLGA)
S.P.F. Standard	(Canadian NLGA)

Joist material

M75	(BS 4978)
SS or MSS	(BS 4978)
S.P.F. No. 1	(Canadian NLGA)
M50	(BS 4978)
GS or MGS	(Canadian NLGA)
S.P.F. No. 2	(BS 4978)

Lintel material

M75	(BS 4978)
SS or MSS	(BS 4978)
S.P.F. No. 1	(Canadian NLGA)
M50	(BS 4978)
GS or MGS	(BS 4978)
S.P.F. No. 2	(Canadian NLGA)

It must be emphasized that these lists are a guide only and, should a specified grade not be available, reference should always be made to the designer.

The most popular species of timber used in the UK timber-frame housing market is known as S.P.F. (spruce, pine, fir) from Canada. However, European redwood/whitewood is often used, especially for the larger-section material for joists and lintels, when the C.L.S. sizes of S.P.F. material can prove uneconomic. The S.P.F. group can include white spruce, Engelmann spruce, red spruce, black spruce, Lodgepole pine, jack pine, alpine fir and balsam fir. The predominant species in any one pack is normally Western white spruce.

Plywood

Plywood is used in timber-frame construction for sheathing external wall panels and for the floor deck. Other sheet materials are sometimes used in these instances but plywood is easily the most commonly used. Again, there are various grades and thicknesses of plywood, and care must be taken to see that the right material is used in its right place. The material should always be external quality and flooring should be tongued and grooved. Sheathing plywood is normally 8 or 9.5 mm sheathing grade square-edged and flooring plywood normally 16 mm T. and G. select sheathing grade. Where a higher standard of finish is required for the flooring, 16 mm T. and G. good one side (G.1.S.) is specified.

Birch-faced plywood is usually specified where painted plywood is used as a cladding material.

Roofs

Roofs for timber-frame dwellings are generally formed of prefabricated truss rafters with in-situ hips, valleys etc., or flat roofs formed of joists with plywood deck to receive the roof-covering material. In other words, roofing a timber-frame house is no different from roofing a traditionally-built house. There is no reason why a timber-frame house should not have a thatched roof if desired.

12

Precautions against infestation and decay

Bugs, beetles, woodworm etc. are not likely to live, nor decay occur, in timber that has a moisture content of 20 per cent or less and such timber, provided it is kept dry and ventilated when built into the structure, will not deteriorate or rot. Generally speaking, treatment of timber against rot and infestation is not, therefore, required in properly detailed and constructed timber-frame housing, except for those timbers in direct contact with the elements or ground conditions, i.e. sole plates, all external battens for roofing and cladding, window frames, door frames, external doors etc. The current Building Regulations also call for roof trusses to be treated when used in certain areas of the country, notably the Surrey/Hampshire borders where long-horn beetles are known to exist.

In addition, where houses are built to comply with the NHBC requirements, further elements have to be treated. Unless the supplier of these treated elements uses a coloured dye in his treatment, it is sometimes difficult to be sure that the elements have, in fact, been treated. If this is the case, a letter certifying that the correct treatment has been applied should always be sought from the supplier.

Care should always be taken to keep treated timbers quite separate from untreated, as untreated top plates can easily be mistaken for, and used as, treated sole plates, and vice versa. Without dye in the treatment, sole plates and top plates appear identical. If, of course, the client can afford to have all the timber treated, this worry disappears and some developers believe that the additional cost for treatment of all timber is well justified as an additional sales aid.

Fire resistance

Fire resistance of timber-frame housing needs to be considered, in order to expel fears in some quarters, due to ignorance of the facts. The roofs and floors of a timber-frame house are constructed almost identically to those of traditional construction. The timber-frame partitions and inner leaves of external walls are all adequately protected against fire by plasterboard, which is a very good fire-resisting material. The Building Regulations call for certain lengths of time of fire resistance before internal flame reaches the timber structural elements and these, which are $\frac{1}{2}$ hour to external walls, 1 hour to party walls etc., are achieved by applying various thicknesses of plasterboard lining.

The spread of fire within cavities is dealt with by fire-stopping at the positions defined in the Building Regulations. Cavities without fire-stopping can act as flues and greatly accelerate the spread of flame. Nearly all fires in homes are caused by accident or stupidity within the house. Over 40 per cent of all domestic fires start in the kitchen, with three-quarters of these started by cooking operations. It is the contents of the home (curtains, furniture, frying pans etc.) which burn, smoulder and give off lethal fumes, and not the actual structure. Modern timber-frame housing has now been in use in the UK since the early 1960s. During these twenty years, the record of fires in, and the maintenance of, timber-frame housing has been carefully watched and monitored. Although, at the beginning of this period, insurance companies and building societies were a little wary, it is fair to say that both now generally treat timber-frame construction on a level with traditional masonry construction.

Life expectancy of timber-frame houses

In Canada and the western states of America, over 90 per cent of all one-family dwellings are constructed in timber frame. In Scandinavia, the figure is 80 per cent. In the UK, at present, the figure is approximately 23 per cent and rising annually. How long will timber-frame houses last? That is a fairly common question asked when discussing timber-frame housing. The answer is that there is no technical or scientific reason why a timber-frame house, properly designed and constructed, will not last as long as the same house properly designed and constructed in traditional masonry. The British Government certainly shares this view. It provides 60-year loan sanction to local authorities who build houses for council tenants, whether they are built by conventional methods or in timber frame.

It is also often asked how long we will be able to carry on felling trees and using timber for construction. In actual fact, timber is one of the few materials that is self-generating. Trees can be felled, and new trees planted, grown and felled in a continuous cycle. The Canadians claim that they are producing 5 per cent more trees every year. In contrast, there must be a limited amount of sand, ballast and clay for bricks. Once it has gone, it has gone for ever. No-one knows when that day will be but we do know that when it arrives, trees will still be growing. It is said that some of the largest deposits of ballast in the UK have been put out of reach by constructing London Airport over them.

2

Substructures

Lightweight structures

Yet another advantage of timber-frame housing over masonry construction is that it is lighter in weight and, therefore, has lighter foundation loading requirements. This makes timber-frame construction highly suitable for suspect ground conditions which are unable economically to support heavier masonry construction. With the shortage of building land in the UK, more and more substandard sites are being used where consulting engineers are advising architects to build in timber-frame because of the inferior ground conditions. This is another reason why timber-frame housing is gaining in popularity in the UK.

Types of foundation

Any type of foundation can be used with timber-frame construction. The overriding and all-important thing to remember is that it is essential to get an accurately dimensioned and level bed under all sole plates, both internal and external. Additional time and care must be allowed to achieve this, as the setting-out, levelling and fixing of the sole plates is the most important operation in the whole of the erection of the timber frame. It stands to reason that, if you are wrong at the bottom, where you start, it is impossible to get your upper structure correct.

A concrete oversite slab sitting on footings is probably the most commonly used substructure. The footings can be of concrete-filled trenches, with the slab formed with the aid of shuttering on top. Concrete strip footings are preferable, rising up with a single skin of brickwork to form permanent shuttering for the slab. The advantages of this method are that the bricklayer is generally able to get his brickwork more accurate and level than the carpenter his shuttering and there is no fear of moving the shuttering during the tamping of the concrete slab. Fixing bricks (to BS 1180) can also be incorporated in the top course to facilitate fixing of sole plates to the external walls, avoiding expensive shot-firing into the concrete.

When tamping the concrete slab across a fairly wide expanse (front to back of house, for example), a saucering effect can be created by the deflection in the tamping board. In these circumstances, the long tamping board must incorporate a slight upward camber to counteract this, as it will be clear that, if the slab saucers in the middle, the sole plates will have to be shimmed to gain a level surface overall for the panels. Once you have shimmed you are into extra labour and materials because, in addition to the shims, the underside of the lengths of sole plate, which are not sitting firmly on the slab, have to be hand-packed with mortar to ensure a solid and continuous bed. If this is not done, the shims will compress into the sole plates when the loading of the super-structure is applied and an uneven sole plate will create disastrous effects. Shims must always be of non-compressible material, such as slate or asbestos cement. Folded d.p.c. or breather paper must never be used. The more shimming required to ensure level sole plates, the more screed will be required because, having secured the sole plates, the slab is screeded up to the top level of them. This is another good reason for taking extra care to secure a level concrete slab.

Contractors embarking on their first timber-frame project are likely to be wary of providing a sand-cement screed which is only a nominal 38 mm thick. Their worries are unfounded, as experienced contractors will confirm. Very little, if any, curling takes place and an excellent job is obtainable.

Before finally fixing sole plates (see Fig. 2.1), it is advisable to set them out and temporarily join them together with corrugated timber fasteners to ensure accurate dimensions and square junctions.

Screeding

Screeding before erection of components is advantageous, although some contractors find this difficult to appreciate when commencing with timber-frame construction. It needs careful planning and organization, as gas carcassing, service entries and drainage outlets have to be located accurately at an early stage, but the overwhelm-

Fig. 2.1 Sole plates fixed to slab before laying of screed.

17

ing advantages include: being the only wet trade inside the dwelling, it dries out more quickly and easily before the shell is erected; it is more economical, because the sole plates can be used as a template on which to level (remember that sole plates occur under every partition wall, as well as under the external wall panels); and a large expanse is open to the screeder without the labour-intensive problem of wheeling his material in barrows through door openings, with consequent risk of damage to linings and frames (see Fig. 2.2). The efficient use of the sole plates as a template, and as a solid support for a levelling and tamping board, may create a more compacted screed, which helps to avoid curling.

When faced with this for the first time, contractors nearly always raise the question of damage to the screed during the building operations. In the author's experience, little or no damage takes place. There are no broken bricks and mortar to fall on it from the inside. It is probably true to say that almost all contractors experienced in timber-frame construction now screed before superstructure erection.

The only exception to this might be on a very large scheme where one terrace of dwellings might be erected before screeding and kept to provide work for the screeders at times of adverse weather conditions.

Sole plates

If the design being followed has a d.p.c. under the sole plates, care must be taken to ensure that the protruding edges of the d.p.c. are turned up and secured by staples to the side of the sole plates. This will prevent moisture from the screed soaking into the sole plates. If the design has the d.p.c. on top of the sole plates then, again, the protruding edges should be turned up and stapled to the sides of the bottom rails of the ground-floor panels. This will prevent any water spillage on the ground floor soaking into the panel.

In cold weather, difficulty may be experienced in bending the d.p.c. at right angles to achieve a good clean turn-up or turn-down. It may be found that heat has to be applied and, therefore, the fixing of the d.p.c. to the sole plates might best be done in a shed on site before they are taken to the slab for fixing. If this procedure is followed, care must be taken to see that sufficient d.p.c. material is left at one end of each sole plate to allow adequate lapping.

The question of penetrating the d.p.c. with fixing nails, either above or below the sole plates, is often raised. It is generally

Fig. 2.2 Screeding in progress.

believed by those experienced, including TRADA, that, provided a bitumastic-based d.p.c. is used, there will be no capillary action up the nail through the d.p.c., as the bitumastic forms a seal round the nail. Despite this, some designers, and some building inspectors, insist on the use of U brackets cast into the slab or brickwork and nailed through into the sides of the sole plates. An alternative to this is to cast into the slab metal straps which are bent over and nailed into the top of the sole plates.

Suspended floors

Suspended ground floors are, of course, possible with timber-frame construction and are formed in exactly the same way as upper floors, except that they sit on dwarf walls capped with sole plates. Except where houses are built on steeply sloping ground, suspended ground floors are generally found to be more expensive than solid-slab construction.

Accuracy

Before leaving substructures, it is worth repeating the importance of accuracy required in setting out, levelling and fixing of sole plates. Besides the checking of running dimensions, diagonal dimensions are of equal importance and the levels must be checked with a levelling instrument. Remember, more time spent on the sole plates can save you considerable time and trouble in the long run.

3

Sequence of building operations

To obtain the full benefits of building timber-frame housing, it has to be realized and appreciated that the sequence of building is quite different from that of traditional construction. A whole new approach is needed from those responsible for programming the job and from the man on site. More careful planning and organization is required to see that the right materials and men are in the right place at the right time. If this is achieved, quite remarkable results can be obtained. A scheme was recently completed of 425 houses in East Anglia for occupation by United States Air Force personnel. These houses were larger than the normal houses built for local authorities and finished to a higher standard, including fitted carpets to the first floor etc. The contract, consisting of 425 houses, all roads and sewers, a bridge, 2 balancing lakes and 2 pumping stations, was completed in 81 weeks. A similar contract of 300 units as seen in Fig. 3.1 was completed in 66 weeks by the same contractor.

Man hours

The calculation of man hours required to erect the timber frame of a two-storey three-bedroom house, i.e. ground-floor panels, top plates, floor joists, plywood floor deck, first-floor panels, top plates and roof trusses, is a first essential to any programme. A rough guide is one man, one two-storey three-bedroom house in one working week. After a short learning curve, this can normally be improved upon and it will be found that four men can erect five such houses in a week. These are superstructures only. In other words, it is after the foundations, ground-floor slab and sole plates are ready to receive the superstructure.

Erectors normally work in gangs of three or four but, on large contracts, it sometimes works out that one gang of three or four

Fig. 3.1 FrameForm timber-frame housing for occupation by USAF personnel. Part of 300-unit scheme in East Anglia completed in 66 weeks by French Keir Construction Ltd.

will erect all the ground–floor panels, top plates and joists, followed by a second gang who fix the plywood floor deck, first-floor panels, first-floor top plates and roof trusses. Very large contracts can be subdivided even further, so that a gang of, say, two men do nothing other than fix floor joists, and become remarkably skilled and fast in the operation. Balancing these subdivisions, to gain a steady and progressive flow of completed structures, needs careful watching and will vary according to the complexity of the design. Steps, staggers, projections and recesses on plan, bay windows etc. all need additional thinking and additional work. They, therefore, take additional time.

Sequence of operations

Given that the ground–floor slab is complete up to sole plate and screed, the sequence of operations to follow for a two-storey three-bedroom house is generally as follows (operations listed against the same sequence number should be carried out simultaneously):

1 Ground–floor panels.
2 Ground–floor top plates.
3 Floor joists.
4 Floor deck.
5 First-floor panels.

6 First-floor top plates.
7 Roof trusses and gable ladders.
8 Scaffold.
9 (a) Soil-and-vent pipe;
  (b) Fascias and rainwater gutters;
  (c) Roof tiling;
  (d) External doors;
  (e) External glazing;
  (f) Breather paper.
10 (a) First-fix plumber and electrician;
  (b) External cladding and rainwater downpipes;
  (c) External painting (unless painter is prepared to work from ladders).
11 Insulation and vapour barrier.
12 Plasterboard tacking; tape-and-fill.
13 Second-fix carpenter, plumber and electrician.
14 Painting and decorating internally.
15 Floor coverings.

Brick chimney breast

If the design incorporates a brick-built chimney breast and flue, it is strongly recommended that this be accurately located on the slab and built at least up to first-floor level before the timber-frame erection is commenced. Where a large breast stops at the underside of the ground-floor ceiling, care must be taken to see that the brick-work stops at least 10 mm below the underside of the floor joists to allow for the shrinkage of timber.

Main differences with traditional counterpart

The sequence set out above will obviously vary slightly according to various conditions, size of contract and claddings to be used. However, it does highlight the main differences between the sequence of trades employed on a traditionally-built house and those employed on timber-frame housing. If a gang of four erectors is employed, it will be seen that, bearing in mind the rough calculation given earlier, from the commencement of erecting super-structures (stage 1), it is only a week before scaffolding for four dwellings is required (stage 8), that is, assuming four men only erect four houses in a week. This is the first apparent major difference from building traditionally: the short time from commencement until full scaffolding is required to enable the roof tiler to begin work. There would appear to be no statutory safety regulations at the moment specifically covering timber-frame erection without scaffolding. It can, therefore, be assumed that the timber-frame erector accepts the hazards of his trade, as do steeplejacks, structural steel-frame erectors and scaffolders.

The glazier also carries out his work at a much earlier stage than in traditional construction.

It will be appreciated that, on completion of stage 9, the dwelling is completely sealed and weathertight, enabling all following trades inside the dwelling to work in dry and warm conditions. This is a great advantage to the man on site.

At the completion of stage 9, the dwelling is also structurally stable. Whatever the cladding, it is purely decorative and in no way can be considered a structural element. Indeed, in Canada, it is not unknown for a family to build its own timber-frame house and commence to live in it while it is still wrapped in breather paper, the claddings being added later as and when they can be afforded.

Scaffolding

The type and timing of scaffolding to be used is a very difficult thing to recommend, as two experienced timber-frame housing contractors seldom have similar ideas on the subject.

Small-panel platform-frame construction (as opposed to large-panel construction, requiring cranage to hoist it into position) can be erected without scaffolding. The problem arises when the dwelling has to be roofed, because roof tilers will not generally tile a roof unless full scaffolding is provided. It is interesting to note here that the only area in the UK where roof tilers have been found who did not insist on full scaffolding, was in the Liverpool area. There, tilers were quite happy to work overhand from the inside, putting the top course and ridge tiles on from ladders on the outside.

To erect full scaffolding at this stage (stage 8), could, if not carefully thought out, hinder work of subsequent trades, i.e. glazing, cladding, application of breather paper etc. One of the ways commonly used to overcome this problem is to erect full scaffolding a short distance away from the timber frame and then use cantilevered brackets on the inside at various levels to suit the various trades. One experienced timber-frame contractor finds it preferable to erect scaffolding for the roof tiler, then dismantle and re-erect as cladding rises. However, the cantilevered bracket system seems preferable to the duplicate erection.

There are now available to timber-frame contractors various forms of hanging scaffold devised to provide scaffolding for the roof tiler which does not have to rise up from the ground level. Hanging scaffold consists generally of an upright pole with a hook at the top and cantilevered brackets to receive scaffold boards. The hooked end is placed over the top-floor top plate and the pole rests against the outside of the top-floor panels or is kept a short distance from the sheathing by means of spacers. The cantilevered brackets incorporate an upstand baluster to hold a handrail/guardrail (see

Fig. 3.2 Kwikform hanging scaffold in course of erection.

Fig. 3.2). On completion of the roof tiling, the supporting pole is unhooked from the wall panel from inside the dwelling by withdrawing a connecting pin or similar. Various manufacturers have devised a number of patent hooks and connections to facilitate this dismantling operation.

While some contractors have used this system quite successfully, the drawbacks include: restricted walkway, with large eaves overhang; difficulty of operation with layouts involving steps and staggers between houses; impossibility of use at gable ends with pitched roofs; careful planning and spacing required to avoid window openings, projecting sills, s.v.ps inside external walls etc.; and, where there are no internal partitions at right angles to the top-floor external panels, the hanging scaffold can bow out the external walls.

Summary of main differences in sequence of operations

To summarize, the main differences in sequence of operations which the site man, working on timber-frame housing for the first time, must appreciate in order to achieve the full advantages are: scaffolding required on site within hours of commencement of panel erection; roof tiler to commence very soon after start of panel erection; and hanging of external doors and glazing of all openings required much earlier than with traditional construction.

Benefits to specialist trades

The well-organized site will find that plumbers, electricians; heating engineers etc. will soon appreciate the benefits of working on a timber-frame housing scheme, where they are able to work in dry and comparatively warm conditions inside the weathertight structure. Another advantage, not generally appreciated until experienced, is that men working inside the dwelling on first-fix are able to walk through walls (i.e. between studs) instead of having to walk further by having to use door openings, as in masonry-built dwellings. Similarly, in terraced housing, men are able to walk from house to house (i.e. between studs of the twin-leaf party wall) without having to go outside in possibly cold and wet conditions. Builders' work in connection with wiring and plumbing does not entail having a labourer to make holes through, and chases in, masonry walls. All these advantages make timber-frame housing more attractive to plumbing, heating and electrical trades. This fact alone can be advantageous to the contractor and his site operatives, especially during times of plenty of work and shortage of labour.

Controlled shell erection

On large sites, once shell erection commences, there is a great temptation to surge forward, putting up shells way ahead of following trades. On contract work, this is encouraged by the terms of the contract, whereby the contractor is paid for materials as they are delivered. Contractors soon find that shell erections can produce quite large certificates of payment at an early stage of the job and so greatly assist cash flow. However, to proceed too quickly with shell erection creates great management and supervision problems, and spreads the site unnecessarily. Ideally, shell erection should go no faster than the slowest trade following.

With houses for sale, builders govern their rate of building to the rate of expected sales, as it is only when houses are sold that cash comes in.

4

Components

Delivery

Manufacturers and suppliers of component parts have various methods of delivery to sites. The one-off house will usually come complete on one load. With large contract work, manufacturers tend to stack panels horizontally in half-house sets, i.e. one set comprising all ground-floor panels, another all first-floor panels etc. A half-house set of a normal three-bedroom house makes a convenient load for a fork-lift truck to facilitate loading and unloading. The usual articulated lorry will carry a load at least two half-houses high, the total number carried being dependent on the length of the trailer. The important thing for the site man to remember is to see that he gets his deliveries in the order he wants. A strongly advocated method is one whereby ground-floor panels are erected for quite a few houses before first-floor panels are delivered. This enables joists and floor decks to be constructed after the first ground-floor panels are up and the first-floor panels, when they arrive, may be placed on the first-floor deck of the appropriate units. This sequence can be seen in operation in Fig. 1.2 and, if carefully planned, it will eliminate double handling of panels, i.e. straight from lorry to first-floor deck rather than from lorry to storage and then from storage to position for erection.

It is not advocated that the whole of the first-floor panels be placed in one stack on the first-floor platform by fork-lift truck straight off the trailer. This causes great congestion in a limited space, as the panels then have to be sorted and placed in their correct positions. With small-panel construction, all panels are capable of being manhandled and can easily be lifted to the first-floor platform individually by hand and placed in position. On a good level site, it is sometimes possible to get the trailers alongside the

28

ground-floor construction to enable panels to be lifted direct from trailer to first-floor location. In long terrace construction, it might be found advantageous to lift the first-floor panels of the first house on to the floor deck of the second house and so on along the terrace. This method overcomes the problem of congestion mentioned above.

Storage and handling of components on site

If panels have to be stored on site before erection, care must be taken to see that they are kept off the ground and level. It is preferable to have an external panel, with its sheathing uppermost, on top of the stack of panels if they are stacked horizontally. This will offer some protection from rain although, on a well-organized site, components should not be stacked on site for any length of time before erection. However, a sheathed external panel with the plywood facing downwards should never be placed on top of a stack of components, enabling rainwater to collect and be retained between the studs.

Joists

Floor joists should be kept well off the ground by use of cross bearers at sufficient intervals to avoid any sagging of the joists. If covered for protection from rain, enough air must be allowed to circulate beneath the covers to permit the timber to breathe. It is prudent to remember, however, that hot sunshine can cause as much, if not more, damage to kiln-dried timber than rain. Rainwater does not penetrate very deeply into timber and soon dries out, provided the timber is well ventilated and not allowed to remain submerged in water.

For comparatively small additional cost, floor joists can be banded together in house or block sets. This can be a great help on site and saves many man hours sorting joists into sets. If house or block sets are used, they must never be allowed to be broken open except for use on the particular house or block. If one joist is borrowed for the house next door and so on, the benefits of having individual sets is soon lost. On large sites, it is recommended that spare sets for each type of house be kept in the compound and used as replacements for any defective joists found in the sets out on site.

Roof trusses

Roof trusses should always be carried, stored and hoisted in an upright position. They should be stored with bearers under the same points at which they are supported when in position on the roof. No part of the truss should be touching the ground and protection should be afforded against rain and sun, as for joists. Simple stands made up from scaffolding are ideal for storage of trusses.

Trusses are usually delivered to site in bundles, strapped tightly together with metal or strong plastic straps. The metal connecting plates on trusses, being face-fixed, mean that the thickness of a bundle of trusses is greatest at the point of the plates. Therefore, the straps should go round the trusses in close proximity to the plates. If they are put round at mid-span, between plates, the timbers are drawn close together, causing distortion, especially to the outside trusses of the bundle. Such distortion will remain in the trusses when erected, causing problems for the roof tiler and ceiling tacker. In any case, the straps should be released as soon as the trusses are off-loaded on site and stored correctly, to prevent their cutting into the timber should the timber swell (see Figs. 4.1 and 4.2).

Trusses should always be manufactured with a slight upward camber in the ceiling joist. This is to allow for the slight deflection in the ceiling joist when the roof is loaded out. In this way, no load is put on the internal first-floor partitions which, generally, are not

Fig. 4.1 Trusses banded together with steel straps round timber members midway between truss plates, causing distortion of timbers.

Fig. 4.2 Another view of same bundle of trusses showing incorrect site stacking and distortion caused by metal strapping. These trusses were condemned.

designed to be loadbearing. Trusses are normally designed to span from external wall to external wall. If the specification calls for the trusses to be nailed to the top of any internal partitions they cross, this can only be done after the roof is loaded and the deflection in the trusses has taken place. After loading, the trusses should then be just touching the tops of the internal walls they cross.

The mechanical plated truss has the prongs of the plates hydraulically pressed into the face of the timbers to secure the joint. It stands to reason that any whip action activated in the truss will tend to weaken the strength of the joint. Indeed, if sufficient whip is put into the truss, the plates can be sprung out of the timber. The handling of trusses is, therefore, of paramount importance. If they are treated like a sheet of plate glass, all will be well.

Plywood

External-quality plywood, when delivered in bulk, comes in packs of forty sheets, normally protected with a cover of thin-plywood and tightly bundled with metal straps. These packs store well externally but if they are stored on site for any time, the metal straps should be cut. This enables the plywood to swell under atmospheric conditions without cutting into the edges of the sheets, so causing damage, especially to the tongues and grooves. Adequate bearers to avoid contact with the ground are, of course, essential.

31

Erection of components

Before commencement of erection, it is worth while to ensure that the sole plates are swept clean, that they are fixed adequately and completely bedded and that the overall dimensions are accurate (see Fig. 4.3.

The team of erectors should be equipped with claw hammers, boxed-out nail pouches round their waists, measuring tapes, level, step ladders, full set of drawings and specifications, and an adequate supply of nails. A large magnet pulled over the floor by a piece of string will save a lot of back bending and time in recovering dropped nails.

When panels are joined together, they should be stitch-nailed, i.e. nails driven in at opposite angles on either side of the two members being nailed together.

Erection of components should commence with two panels forming an external corner and should continue in both directions until an internal wall panel is reached that meets the externals at right angles. At least one of these internal panels should be erected to assist bracing the externals before the internal panels are erected as a whole. If, in a particular design, there is a long length of external wall without an internal wall at right angles, some form of temporary bracing may be required until the whole structure is plumbed and completed (see Fig. 4.4).

On completion of the ground-floor components, including final plumbing and nailing, the top plates have to be secured as shown in Fig. 4.5. The fixing nails should never be driven straight into the timber, always at an angle (skew-nailed) and always staggered down the length of timber to avoid the possibility of splitting.

If the design calls for a straight-flight internal staircase, ensure that it can be installed after the structure is up. Some designs, especially those with a straight-flight staircase in the middle of the ground floor at right angles to the side walls, do not allow this, in which case, the staircase must be installed with the ground-floor components.

Floor joists generally arrive on site cut to length. They are laid out on a module to suit plasterboard and plywood dimensions. Unlike traditional construction, where ends of floor joists meet over a loadbearing wall, the ends are butted together and 'scabbed' or faced with a piece of plywood or metal nailed truss plate to assist in keeping the two ends in the same plane. Scabbing with truss plates can be seen in Fig. 6.2. If the joists were to pass each other

Fig. 4.3   Service entries and screeding complete, ready for erection of ground-floor panels.

Fig. 4.4 Commencement of erection of ground-floor components.

34

Fig. 4.5 Ground-floor components complete with top plates.

Fig. 4.6 Commencement of fixing in position of floor joists cut to length.

as in traditional construction, they would obviously go off module (see Fig. 4.6).

As in all forms of good construction, any crown in the joists should be uppermost. If the specification calls for joists to be 'toe-nailed' into the top plates, great care must be taken to avoid split-ting the edges of the joist. Galvanized metal joist clips are now available which greatly reduce the chances of split joists.

Sometimes, designers will incorporate flitch lintels into the design of the floor in order to cope economically with wide spans. A flitch lintel can span at right angles to floor joists, which will hang on either side by means of joist hangers. The flitch lintel will probably be formed of two joists bolted together, with a steel plate between the two. As the depth of the joists will inevitably shrink, it is important to see that the depth of the steel plate is less than the joist depth and that the timber oversails the steel top and bottom.

Tongued-and-grooved sheet material for floor deck must always be laid at right angles to the floor joists and annular-ringed shank nails used for its fixing. A complete pack of forty sheets of ply-wood should never be lifted and placed in one stack on the floor joists before fixing, as the weight would exceed the domestic floor loading provided.

First-floor panels and top plates are erected as for the ground floor (see Fig. 4.7). It might, however, prove advantageous to leave one external window panel unfixed to facilitate passing up the roof trusses by hand, keeping them vertical. The first end of the truss can be placed on the top plate of the opposite wall and the other end lifted on to the top plate adjacent to the omitted window panel. Still in an upright position, the trusses can then be stacked to one side of the opening, pending spacing and fixing after the window panel and top plate have been fixed. A window panel is recommended because the opening provides the facility for the erector to locate the last panel by leaning through the opening and tapping it into position from the outside. Some contractors find they can pass up the roof trusses through the cavity of the party wall. The spacing of the trusses can easily be marked on the top of the top plates or a spacing stick can be used. A pre-nailed tem-porary batten should also be marked with the correct spacing and used near the apex of the trusses to see that they are kept upright, as can be seen in Fig. 4.8. Before final fixing of roof trusses and all specified bracing, a check should be made to ensure that any cold-water storage tank or storage platform specified will, in fact,

Fig. 4.7 Erection of first-floor components in progress.

Fig. 4.8 Roof trusses being fixed and held upright by temporary batten near ridge, pending fixing of truss bracing and roof tiling battens.

pass through the proposed ceiling hatch. If it will not, then it must be inserted in the roof space before the final truss is fixed. For ease of working, it is strongly recommended that tank supports etc. in the roof space be fixed before roof tiling.

Flat-roofs

Flat-roof construction is achieved in exactly the same way as inter-mediate floor construction except that falls to the sheet material are provided by placing firring pieces of timber on top of the joists. With flat-roof construction, there are two important points to remember. Firstly, the roofing joists must be well ventilated to the outside air. If joists run at right angles to the external wall, holes must be drilled in the header joist centrally between supporting joists. If the joists run parallel to the external wall, each and every joist should be drilled in the neutral axis at, say, 600 mm centres or as specified by the designer. This is essential to enable the flat roof timbers to breathe, as they will normally be covered on the underside by an impervious vapour barrier and on the top side by an impervious roof covering. The importance for all structural timber of being allowed to breathe is covered in Chapters 5 and 7. Secondly, if a parapet wall surrounds the flat roof, the upstand of the flat-roof covering material must be covered with a flashing. This must come down from the parapet in such a manner as to allow for the upstand to slide down behind the flashing when the roof joists shrink, the upstand still remaining adequately covered by the flashing. This is known as counterflashing.

Noggings, fire-stop blockings etc.

If the design calls for site-fixed noggings and blockings, these should be fixed immediately the panels are erected. The position of the blockings will be shown on the drawings but noggings will have to be located according to the fixing requirements of the kitchen fittings, sanitary fittings, electrical fittings etc. Very careful liaison with all these trades is essential. On large sites, the site management can benefit greatly by preparing their own nogging drawings, showing the total requirement for each house type. Early consideration and determination of nogging positions is essential, as they must be nailed in position as the panels go up to avoid delays in commencement of following sequences. Insulation, for example, cannot be inserted in external wall panels until after the noggings are fixed.

It is also worth mentioning here that, although centres of studs, joists and trusses may all generally be set out at 600 mm, pre-cut noggings will probably have to be three different lengths because of the different thicknesses of the timber used for the three purposes. For example, studs might be at 38 mm, joists at 44 mm and trusses at 35 mm. Standard noggings would, therefore, be 562 mm, 556 mm and 565 mm in length. Care must be taken to keep these carefully identified and used only for the purpose intended. It has often been claimed that noggings were delivered too long and were having to be cut on site, until it was pointed out that stud noggings were being used for joists.

5

Making the shell weathertight

The timber frame having been erected, several trades can now be brought in to work concurrently to render the dwelling weathertight.

Roof tiler
Roof tiling can commence immediately scaffolding is erected.

Plumber
The plumber will need to erect the soil and ventilation pipe to enable the roof tiler to complete his work.

Glazier
The glazier can carry out his external glazing, utilizing the scaffolding erected for the roof tiler.

Carpenter
The carpenter can hang the external doors.

Application of breather paper

Some designers rely on the external quality of the sheathing material to keep the main shell weathertight. This is not recommended because the sheathing material is only butt-jointed, and these joints can allow water penetration into the frames during the period before the cladding is applied. Good practice for timber-frame construction is to cover the whole of the external face of the timber-frame walls with a breather paper to form a moisture barrier. Breather paper is manufactured in rolls like roofing felt and is stapled to the sheathing in horizontal layers, starting at the bottom of the house and lapping each course, top over bottom, by at least 100 mm. The bottom run of breather paper should be extended downwards to protect adequately the exposed edge of the sole plate beneath the external components.

A hammer-type stapler has proved the best instrument for fixing breather paper but great care must be taken to avoid random stapling. It is important that the staples coincide with the staple or nail fixings in the sheathing material, that is, through the sheathing and into the studs. If this is carefully carried out as the breather paper is unrolled round the unit, it facilitates location and fixing of brick ties, battens for cladding fixings etc. so that nails go through into the studs. That is to say, fixing nails for brick ties and battens are located over staples in breather paper, and staples in breather paper are located over fixings in sheathing material which, in turn, are fixed into the studs.

The breather paper, or moisture barrier as it is sometimes known, must be a breather-type building paper conforming to BS 4016: 1966. Although providing a barrier to keep moisture out of the timber frame from the outside, it does allow moisture under pressure to pass and the timber frame to breathe through it. It, therefore, has two functions. The first is to protect and weatherproof the house immediately after erection of the shell, and to provide a secondary line of defence against the penetration of wind-driven rain or moisture which may find its way through the exterior cladding materials. The second is to allow the escape of any moisture vapour which finds its way through the inner barrier or which is residual in the timber framing.

If the timber-frame shells are left for some time just wrapped in the breather paper before claddings are applied, damage to the breather paper can be caused by winds, especially on exposed sites. It is, therefore, essential to use a robust breather paper and ensure that it is adequately stapled. Some success is being achieved at the moment by stapling the breather paper through a narrow band of plastic tape. Besides assisting in keeping the staples in a straight line, it prevents the staples from pulling through the plastic tape as easily as they do through the breather paper. Cheap breather paper and inadequate stapling is a false economy.

Some designers have breather paper applied in the factory to each individual panel. When this is done, extra care must be exercised in handling the components to avoid tearing the breather paper and to ensure that cover strips are site-applied to all joints, properly lapped top over bottom. Fixing the cover strips can hide the true line of staples, masking the position of studs for fixing purposes, which is another disadvantage of factory-applied breather paper.

6

Plumber, heating engineer and electrician

Plumber and heating engineer

The accuracy of site dimensions obtained with timber-frame construction, when components are made off-site in factory conditions, should soon convince the plumber and heating engineer (normally the same tradesman when a wet system of heating is employed) that he can safely prefabricate his main pipe runs. If prefabricated, pipes that run through the floor zone can be dropped into notches in the top of the joists during construction, i.e. immediately before laying the floor deck. Plumbers and heating engineers find this much easier than working on the underside of joists after the shell is completed. In order not to delay the shell erection, however, it is imperative that the pipe runs are prefabricated and are ready for fixing at the correct time. The installer of the pipes must work as a member of the shell erection team. If pipe runs are notched on top of the joists, it is strongly recommended that the location of the runs is pencilled on top of the floor deck to prevent nails from puncturing the pipes during the fixing of the deck material. Similarly, if the pipe runs are notched on the underside of the joists, the plasterboard ceiling boards should be so marked for the same reason. A little care and attention in this direction could save no end of troubles later.

Too much care cannot be exercised in notching joists. It must be remembered that the whole timber shell has been engineered and calculations produced to prove its adequacy. Notching cannot, therefore, be carried out at random but only in accordance with the precise limits set by the designer or engineer. Generally speaking, they should never be more than 25 mm deep and located within the end quarter of the span. This, however, is a generality and each designer will specify the limits he can allow in his design.

A piece of felt or sacking between hot-water pipes and floor joists

44

where they cross will assist in preventing those annoying noises that can occur as pipes within a dwelling commence to get hot and, again, when they cool off.

The largest single problem on handovers is probably water leaks and they can be very costly to cure in time, money and inconvenience to the occupier – taking down ceilings; drying out the structure, furniture, carpets etc.; repairing the leak; and renewing ceilings and redecorating. Sometimes, a nail driven into a pipe will not show a leak for some time, especially with an angular-ringed shank nail. Until the pipe gets hot and expands, the nail will sometimes seal the hole sufficiently to conceal the leak for a considerable time before it becomes apparent on the surface. (Fig. 6.1).

Where cold-water pipes are run in close proximity to hot-water pipes in the floor zone, the latter should be lagged to prevent the cold water from becoming warm, to prevent heat loss and to minimize the risk of surface condensation on the cold-water pipes. In the roof space, all water pipes should be individually lagged and the overflow pipe drop straight down from the tank and fall to the outside within the depth of the ceiling joist, to which it can be clipped. If the overflow pipe runs straight from the tank to the discharge point, it forms an additional hazard in the limited amount

Fig. 6.1 Here plumber has drilled holes through neutral axis of joists
to receive short lengths of water pipe as for electrical wiring.
This is a much safer way than notching as it eliminates risk of
penetration of pipes by fixing nails of plasterboard ceiling or
plywood floor deck.

45

of manoeuvring area within the roof space formed by prefabricated roof trusses. Plastic overflows also tend to sag considerably because of the inability to provide adequate clipping. Another point here to remember is that, if showers are to be provided on the top floor of the house, it is advantageous to place the cold-water storage tank as high as possible within the roof space, thus giving a larger head of water and, therefore, more pressure at the shower outlet.

Timber floor joists in all forms of construction shrink in their depth after installation and further drying out. This is evidenced in a traditionally-built house, soon after occupation, by a gap which appears between the top of the bath and the underside of the wall tiling. This does not happen in a timber platform-frame house because the internal partitions and inner leaf of the external walls all sit on the floor deck so that, as the joists shrink, bath and walls go down together. Nevertheless, it is important to see that the joint between the top of the bath and the underside of the tiles is well waterproofed with one of the proprietary brands of silicone sealing compound available for this purpose, to avoid possible ingress of water into the timber structural frame.

Before leaving the plumber and heating engineer, it is important to mention an often disregarded point of construction. Bearers at right angles to the joists and spanning over at least two joists must be placed under each leg of the bath and, if the hot-water cylinder stands on the floor deck, it should rest on two bearers at right angles to the joists and spanning over at least two. If the legs of a bath are allowed to rest directly on the plywood floor deck, they could occur midway between floor joists, causing considerable deflection and a consequential breakdown of the seal between the top of the bath and the underside of the wall tiling.

There are plumbing and heating installations, generally only in one-off houses, where the installers have gone to great lengths to conceal all water pipes and, sometimes, even waste pipes. Apart from its being contrary to most, if not all, water regulations and good building practice, the resultant notching of studs to accommodate horizontal runs can have catastrophic effects on the sufficiency of the structural design, cause additional hazards for leaks when nailing plasterboard and create great upheaval in locating and repairing leaks occurring after a house is occupied.

Most manufacturers of plastic waste pipes, rainwater pipes and s.v.ps print their name, BS number etc. in a contrasting colour in one continuous line along the length of each piece of pipe produced. When fixing these pipes, it is quite easy to ensure that the line of printing is turned towards the surface to which it is being fixed and thus become hidden from view. This is a small point to consider but it is surprising how often black rainwater pipes can be seen with white lettering running down their full length and white waste pipes from lavatory basins in bathrooms running to a duct with red lettering fully visible.

Electrician

Generally speaking, the electrician finds the wiring of a timber-frame house easier than the wiring of its traditional counterpart. Apart from working in better conditions, as explained in an earlier chapter, drilling holes in timber and fixing switch boxes and socket outlets to timber noggings is much easier than drilling holes in, and fixing fittings to, masonry.

When wiring is run in the floor zone at right angles to the joists, it should be run through holes drilled in the neutral axis of the joists. The size and positions of the holes should be in accordance with the limits set by the designer. Where the wiring runs parallel to the joists, it should be adequately stapled to the sides of the joists

Fig. 6.2 Wiring clipped to side of floor joists, clear of edges to avoid possible penetration by ceiling plasterboard and floor-deck nailing.

well clear of the top and bottom edges, where it can be safe from any nailing of the floor deck and plasterboard ceiling. See Fig. 6.2. In the roof space, truss members should never be drilled and the stapling of the wiring to the sides of the trusses should be done with the same strict caution as for the floor joists. The wiring must be clear of the range of the ceiling plasterboard nails which sometimes miss in fixing to the ceiling joist of the truss.

Care must always be taken to ensure that all wiring is kept clear of hot-water pipe runs. Although this is a rule of good practice in all forms of construction, site operatives sometimes become over-enthusiastic when they experience the speed with which they can work with timber-frame housing. Such enthusiasm is to be encouraged but has to be carefully monitored. An example is where the electrician finds he can thread his wiring through the same holes or notches that the plumber has used for his hot-water pipe.

Electrical outlets in external and load-bearing walls have to be fire-stopped. This is normally achieved by fixing 38 mm thick timber or 2 pieces of 12.7 mm plasterboard the full width and depth between studs top and bottom of nogging holding electrical outlet box as shown in Fig. 6.3.

Fig. 6.3 Wiring to socket outlets. Plasterboard blockings top and bottom of nogging is one way of providing necessary fire-stopping.

7

Insulation, vapour barrier and condensation

Before any covering-in of the inside of the components takes place, a check must be made, with the aid of a moisture meter, to see that the moisture content of the timber is 20 per cent or below. When timber is below 20 per cent moisture content, the possibility of fungal attack and decay is negligible. Studs at the sides of external openings and bottom rails of panels are most likely to have the highest moisture content and they, therefore, should be the locations to check. If the correct timber is specified and supplied, and if it has not been stored uncovered for an exceptionally long period in bad weather, the chances of a moisture content over 20 per cent are remote. Should it be in excess, given good weather with windows and doors left open by day, the moisture content will soon drop to the acceptable level.

Insulation

Paper-backed insulation quilt with selvedged edges (see Fig. 7.1) is made to suit stud centres commonly used in timber-frame construction. The spaces between studs are covered with the insulation which is face-fixed by staples through the paper-backed selvedged edges into the face of the studs (see Fig. 7.2). Great care should be taken when cutting the insulation to suit the height of the timber panels to ensure that it is not cut short, leaving a cold bridge at the top or bottom. It is far better for it to be cut a little too long than too short as the surplus can always be tucked in. If the fixers of the insulation are provided with a trestle table, standard full-height lengths of insulation can be pre-cut more accurately than fixing straight from the roll and cutting off at the bottom with a knife. The insulation should always be on the warm side of the wall it is protecting, i.e. never push it back between the studs to rest on the inside face of the sheathing. The paper-backed insulation face-

Fig. 7.1 Roll of Rocksil Timberfill PFl insulation quilt to suit studs at 600 mm centres. Projecting paper edges for stapling into face of studs can be seen.

fixed to the edge of the studs ensures that it is kept in the correct location, normally 80 mm thick to fit a cavity 89 mm deep.

Other forms of insulation placed between studs are available but the paper-backed insulation quilt is the most commonly used and the best for the purpose.

Ceiling insulation in roof spaces is exactly as for masonry construction. It can be of varying thicknesses from 80 mm upwards and there is a variety of materials available, such as Rocksil or

Fig. 7.2 Timberfil PFl being stapled between studs, using a grip
stapling machine.

Fibreglass quilt which is rolled out between trusses (see Fig. 7.3),
loose vermiculite spread between trusses and patent foams blown
into position by mechanical means.

Thermal insulation is provided to prevent heat loss, thus conserving the energy to provide the heat within the dwelling. The
heat loss through building elements is measured by a U value in
units of watts per square metre per degree centigrade (W/m² °C)
temperature difference from face to face of the element. The lower
the U value, the lower the heat loss. The Building Regulations now
require, a minimum U value through external walls of all houses
of 0.6 W/m² °C. A normal timber-frame house with 80 mm insulation between studs, plywood sheathing and brick cladding will
provide a U value of 0.4 W/m² °C.

Fig. 7.3 Rocksil Insulation Quilt being laid in roof space.

Vapour barrier

The vapour barrier which covers the internal face of the whole of the external walls, party walls and top-floor ceiling must be of an impervious sheet material, usually 250 gauge (0.06 mm) low-density polythene membrane to BS 3012: 1970. It should be well lapped at all joints at least 100 mm and adequately stapled to the face of studs and plates, and to the underside of the roof trusses. Great care must be taken to ensure a complete seal and, where openings have to be provided for switch boxes etc., they must not be cut so large as to allow a leakage and discontinuity of the vapour barrier.

The vapour barrier is placed on the warm side of the insulated walls and top ceiling, directly behind the plasterboard linings, to minimize the passage of water vapour from the interior of the house into the structure. A moisture content in the timber of 20 per cent or less and the standard of thermal insulation is thus maintained. British Gypsum market a drywall sealer known as Gyproc Drywall Top Coat. When two coats of this sealer are applied by brush or roller, the manufacturer claims that it achieves a water-vapour resistance that exceeds the generally accepted minimum value for a vapour barrier. Drywall Top Coat is, therefore, claimed by the manufacturer to replace the more conventional polythene vapour barrier, the slurry cost of the dry-lining process and a sealer to the plasterboard should one be required. Against these savings is the cost of supplying and applying two coats of Drywall Top Coat. The author has not yet experienced this material and cannot, therefore, give an opinion.

Condensation

Considerable quantities of water vapour are added to the indoor air by normal household activities such as cooking, laundering, bathing, paraffin heaters etc. This produces an internal vapour pressure higher than that outdoors, with the result that high-pressure vapour builds up indoors and tends to flow to the lower pressure outdoors. If the vapour is allowed to flow through a well-insulated wall, it will condense on the colder regions within the wall. This is known as interstitial condensation.

When this vapour hits a cold solid masonry wall or a cold sheet of glass in a window, it immediately condenses on the surface. This is known as surface condensation. The well-insulated timber-frame construction provides a warm inner surface and the vapour barrier is provided to prevent the water vapour from passing through the warm areas to reach the cold areas. Here, it would condense within the wall structure, causing the moisture content of the timber structure to rise after every effort has been made to ensure that it is below 20 per cent before being sealed in.

Considerable thought has been given to the problem of condensation in timber-frame housing design and the problem has virtually been eliminated. It still remains important, however, for the occupants to realize that condensation will always occur where warm and moist internal air is in contact with cold inside surfaces, such as a single sheet of glass in a window. This often leads to water running down the glass, staining the window frame and causing mould growth. Occupiers of houses often refer to this as leaking windows. Ventilation is, at all times, a prerequisite of a

53

Fig. 7.4 Paper-faced Timberfil insulation fixed to internal walls and polythene-backed Timberfil being fixed with hammer stapler to external walls, eliminating need for vapour barrier.

condensation-free house and this must be realized by occupants, despite the need for heat conservation.

The Building Research Establishment has published an Information Paper on this subject, reference IP 1/81.

We have seen the importance of a completely impervious vapour barrier on the inside face of external timber-frame wall units and the underside of roof trusses. Although the polythene vapour barrier is not completely satisfactory, due to the perforations that have to be made for electrical and plumbing fittings, it is, nevertheless, better than foil-backed plasterboard and polythene-faced wall insulation. The foil on the former is easily scratched and damaged. With the latter, it is far more difficult to cut the insulation and polythene combined to give a tight fit round penetrating fittings. There is far more jointing in both systems, providing the possibility of leaks (Fig. 7.4).

8

Claddings

Brick cladding

Brick cladding is probably the type most often used in the UK. This is no doubt because it requires virtually no maintenance and has stood the test of time. It would also appear to be easier to market a brick-clad timber-frame house because, to the layman, it does not look any different from the traditionally-built house. It is interesting to note in this connection that, while all the major housing developers in this country have turned to timber-frame construction, they seldom mention the method of construction in their advertising and brochures. They advertise the high insulation values and consequent fuel conservation values of their houses but they do not specifically state how this is achieved. Presumably, this is for marketing reasons and, perhaps, will change when timber-frame construction becomes the traditional form of construction for houses in the UK.

To get back to brick cladding, this is applied one half-brick thick with a cavity, usually of 25 mm, between brickwork and timber frame. Some designers specify a 50 mm cavity but 25 mm is generally considered adequate and is normal in North America. The brick cladding is tied to the timber frame with flexible brick ties which are nailed with two 30 mm square twisted nails through into each stud at every fifth course of brickwork. The lower of the two nails must be located as near as possible to the bend of the brick tie, the material of which the NHBC and, by inference, the latest Building Regulations demand to be stainless steel. This means that the fixing nails also have to be in stainless steel. As pointed out before, the timber-frame structure will shrink slightly after occupation and the application of the central heating. The brick cladding will not shrink, hence the necessity for flexible ties to allow for this differential movement. For the same reason, the top of the brick cladding should not finish tight up under any part of the timber-frame structure, that is, gable ladders, trusses forming eaves overhang etc. A gap of at least 10 mm should be left between the top of brickwork and the underside of any timber forming part of the timber-frame structure.

Careful setting out by the bricklayer before he commences is most important. Although it is fair to say that he has a template to work to and does not need to bother about dimensions except for his cavity, he should plumb down from the upper windows to ensure that the reveals are, in fact, dead in line, if that is what is required by the drawings. He must also check distances between joinery items to see how they will affect his bonding, because modules of measurement used in timber-frame design do not always suit brick dimensions. Coursing must be checked to ensure that window sills and heads are met correctly. Unlike masonry construction, windows are set in position before the bricklayer commences. He is, therefore, set a different problem, with which the good designer will help by providing the correct dimensioned heights of sills and heads. The importance for the timber-frame structure to be plumb and true soon becomes apparent when the brick cladding rises. What starts off as a 25 mm cavity at the bottom can disappear or double in size by the time the bricklayer reaches second-floor level if the structure is not plumb. This will, of course, produce serious problems where the brickwork passes projecting window and door frames set in the timber frame.

Vertical joints should be raked out at 900 mm centres and left clean in the course of brickwork immediately below d.p.c. to allow free circulation of air behind the brick cladding and to allow the timber frame to breathe as shown in Fig. 8.1. Similar open joints should be provided above horizontal cavity barriers at joist level.

In long terraces of houses with continuous clay-brick cladding, care must be taken to provide expansion joints in the brickwork at every 12 m. If there are projections or staggers on plan, a straight vertical joint can easily and unobtrusively be provided in the corner of the internal angle. When a completely flat elevation, a 10 mm wide straight joint filled with mastic behind the rainwater downpipe is a good way of complying with the recommendations of BRE Digest No. 65 – *The Selection of Clay Building Bricks*.

Cavity barriers and fire-stopping

Barriers have to be inserted in the cavity in certain positions stipu-

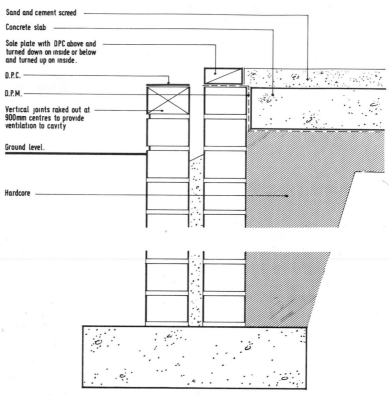

Sand and cement screed

Concrete slab

Sole plate with DPC above and
turned down on inside or below
and turned up on inside.

D.P.C.

D.P.M.

Vertical joints raked out at
900mm centres to provide
ventilation to cavity

Ground level.

Hardcore

Fig. 8.1 Section through typical foundation showing position of
ventilation gaps in bottom of brickwork.

lated by the Building Regulations. Generally speaking, these are
around all openings, horizontally at joist and eaves level and vertically to break up large areas of cavity. The material used for the
cavity barriers is normally an incombustible cavity-fill quilt which
must not be confused with a similar-looking material used for roof
insulation, known as insulation quilt. It is recommended that the
cavity-fill material is fixed in its correct position by a carpenter or
labourer immediately before the bricklayer begins. The same principle applies to the fire-stopping at party walls. It is unreasonable
to expect the bricklayers to fix the cavity barriers and fire-stopping
as they proceed. Indeed, a careful watch has to be kept to see that
these are not dislodged or even removed by the bricklayer as he
works.

These cavity barriers apply to all claddings not directly fixed to
the sheathing.

58

Timber cladding

Any form of timber cladding may be used, vertical, horizontal or diagonal. It is generally applied to 22 × 38 mm treated battens, fixed at right angles to the finished boarding, except for diagonal boarding, where the battens can be either vertical or horizontal. In all cases, the battens must be secured through into the studs. With vertical cladding and horizontal battens, care should be taken to leave 10–20 mm gaps between butt ends of the battens to ensure a circulation of air between breather paper and back of cladding.

Some designers are allowing timber cladding to be applied direct to the breather paper. Adequate insulation value can be achieved, to reach the minimum standards required by the Building Regulations, by the insulation in the external panels of the timber-frame. However, it will be realized that, with vertical cladding, most of the boards will be fixed only to the sheathing. This is acceptable if galvanized or sheradized annular-ringed shank nails are used.

Timber cladding at upper-floor level over brickwork at ground floor is a very common combination in the UK. Care must be taken to see that the timber cladding is not fixed tight to the top of the brickwork. Again, we have the classic case of differential movement. The brickwork rising from the ground will not move. The cladding hanging from the timber frame at upper-floor level will move downwards as the floor joists shrink. The space between the bottom of the timber cladding and the top of the brickwork is detailed by designers in many different ways but the detail must provide a waterproof joint to prevent water ingress into the cavity behind the brickwork. This is generally achieved with mastic or Compriband.

Tile hanging

Horizontal battens fixed as for vertical boarding are essential for tile hanging. Apart from this, there is absolutely no difference from tile hanging on masonry. Some designers have successfully used timber sprockets at the junction of tile hanging over brickwork, so that the bottom course of tiles overlaps the top of the brickwork. This is acceptable in small infill areas but, if a whole house or block has all tile hanging over ground-floor brickwork, complications are met at external corners and it can become quite unsightly. See Fig. 8.2.

Fig. 8.2 House at Fort George, Guernsey, designed by G. M. Bramall and Partners in FrameForm timber-frame construction with components manufactured by Norman Piette Ltd. Claddings used include tile hanging, granite, vertical timber boarding and rendering.

Rendering

Rendering is normally applied to some form of patent lathing fixed to battens, as for the other claddings previously mentioned. The best types of lathing are those that incorporate a waterproof paper back to the galvanized wire mesh. This backing prevents the filling of the cavity created by the battens behind the lathing. By maintaining the cavity, the insulation value of the external wall is increased and, incidentally, material saved, thus decreasing the weight.

Great care should be taken in fixing the lathing, which must always be carried out strictly in accordance with manufacturers' instructions. Apparent little points are sometimes missed, such as the twisting together of the wires when jointing sheets of lathing, instead of just lapping the sheets. With Twil Lath, it is also important to see that the galvanized wires that have a thin stainless-steel wire wrapped round them are used as fixing wires. Rust-resisting staples should always be used for fixing.

Render on lathing on battens, provided it is applied correctly, can be a very effective cladding. The most vulnerable part is where there is an external angle. Operatives tend to bend the lathing through 90 degrees by hand and, therefore, do not get a sharp angle, with consequent loss of rendering material which is applied with a true 90° angle. Where this occurs, cracking often appears. The lathing must be hammered to a true and sharp 90° before fixing or a special corner reinforcement lath utilized.

Extensive rendering on a timber-frame housing contract can delay completions considerably. The fixing of battens and lathing is followed by two, and sometimes three, separate and distinct operations with a drying-out time after each. Apart from the timing of these operations being dictated by weather conditions, scaffolding is utilized for a much longer period than for any other form of cladding.

Maximum areas of rendering without expansion joints are set out in BS 5262: 1976. Where vertical expansion joints are required, they are best located behind rainwater pipes wherever possible.

If the designer has proposed render on blockwork or on brickwork, care must be taken to ensure that this does not meet window and door frames in the reveals of the openings. Differential movement between the timber frame and the masonry will inevitably cause cracking, unless steps are taken to keep these two elements apart. This can be achieved by inserting a temporary piece of hard-

Fig. 8.3 Timber-frame bungalow in Guernsey clad in rendering on Twil Lath. Designed in FrameForm construction by D. R. Jehan.

Fig. 8.4 Timber-frame house in Jersey. Cladding to first floor is rendering on blockwork with artificial quoins formed in rendering.

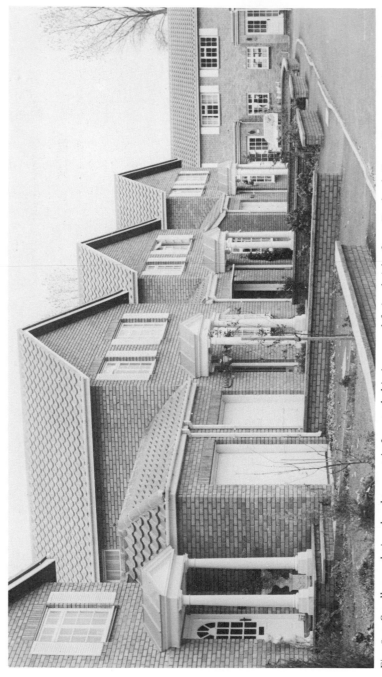

Fig. 8.5 Small speculative development in Jersey clad in imported facing bricks from England. FrameForm components manufactured by Norman Ltd. and development by North Jersey Construction Ltd.

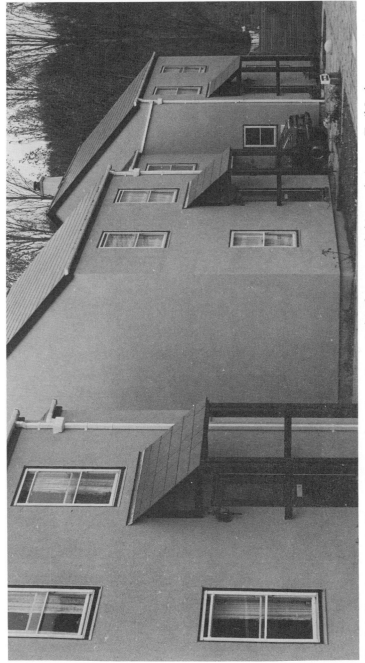

Fig. 8.6 Development in Gorey, Jersey, where FrameForm timber frames are clad in rendering on Twil Lath.

Fig. 8.7 Cladding of timber-frame houses in Jersey painted blockwork with quoins picked out in different colour.

Fig. 8.8 Rendering on blockwork with granite quoins to entrance to timber-frame chalet bungalow in Guernsey.

board strip between the end of the render and the joinery frame. When the render is set, the hardboard strips should be withdrawn and the gaps left behind sealed with a mastic to allow for the differential movement between the timber frame and the rendering.

Sheet materials

Any form of exterior-quality sheet material, finished in a variety of ways, can be used for relatively small infill panels, usually above and below windows. Battens for these panels are fixed as previously described for timber cladding. Great care must be taken to see that the edges of the sheets are well protected and that there is a watertight joint between sheets and adjacent claddings and, if these are of masonry, allowance must be made for differential movement.

Patent claddings

Stove-enamelled aluminium or steel siding, asbestos-cement shingles, plastic siding etc. can all be used if fixed to manufacturers' instructions but, again, the same strict caution must be exercised where two different claddings meet on the same plane.

9

Dry lining

Dry lining describes the internal finish to walls and ceilings achieved by nailing large sheets of plasterboard to the timber structure and filling the joints and nail heads with a water-based joint cement, using a minimum amount of water.

Types of plasterboard used.

The finishing sheets of 12.7 mm Gyproc wallboard have their long edges tapered to accommodate the jointing process and leave a flat and level finish. These boards are known as tapered-edge boards.

When 12.7 mm Gyproc wallboard is specified for ceilings where, ultimately, there is to be a patent plastic-based finish such as Artex, square-edge is sufficient and, of course, cheaper than tapered-edge.

19 mm Gyproc plank is used behind the 12.7 mm wallboard to achieve, where required, 1-hour fire resistance to the structure they are protecting.

Storage of plasterboard

Storage of plasterboard on site is of paramount importance, as it is easily damaged by impact and can be ruined by water saturation. Therefore, it has to be handled carefully, kept well clear of the ground and adequately covered, leaving an air space clear between the ground and the bottom of the covering sheet.

Loading-out

If loading-out is done as a separate operation before the tacking, care must be taken not to overload upper floors which, in accordance with the Building Regulations, are designed for a loading of 1.5 kN/m^2 (approximately 30 lb/ft^2). Unless this is carefully monitored, labourers tend to put all the plasterboard required for the first floor in one stack in the middle of the largest room, grossly overloading the floor and causing considerable deflection in the joists. Even after the load is removed, the joists seldom return to their original level. It is usually wise to put not more than fourteen sheets of 12.7 mm plasterboard in any one stack. If more are required to be stored in a room area, a few can be stood on edge around the perimeter, leaning back on the stud walls.

Tacking

Tacking is sometimes carried out by carpenters and sometimes by the jointers. It is best for the work to be done by the jointers if for no other reason than that it avoids a divided responsibility for a good complete dry-lining job. No matter how good everything else is in a house, if you have not achieved a good dry-lining finish you have not achieved a good job.

The tacker should be equipped with a measuring tape, pencil, metal straight-edge, sharp Stanley knife, boxed waist pouch for nails and a tacker's hammer. This has a slightly domed and scored head which creates a slight scored dimple in the plasterboard when the nail is driven in just below the surface without breaking the paper finish to the plasterboard. The scored dimple forms a key for the nail filling.

In terraced housing, two layers of plasterboard are usually specified for both internal faces of party walls, 12.7 mm tapered-edge plasterboard over 19 mm Gyproc plank. This necessitates fixing the 19 mm plank as the first operation. This same material is sometimes specified for application to the spandril party wall in the roof space. If this is so, it is far easier to fix this before the top-floor ceiling is in position. In order to achieve the necessary 1-hour fire resistance to the party wall, the two layers of plasterboard must have their joints staggered. As it has grown customary in the UK to apply the 12.7 mm plasterboard finish vertically, it is advisable to apply the 19 mm plank horizontally.

Ceilings should be tacked next and should be so set out that the short ends and cut ends of boards are staggered. Wall boards are fixed last and a 3 mm gap should be kept between adjacent tapered edges. They should fit tight under the ceiling boards and be clear of the floor finish by about 15 mm. This 15 mm gap at the bottom is to prevent any water spillage on the floor from soaking up into the plasterboard. The tacker usually uses two small pieces of timber, one at right angles on top of the other. By resting the bottom of the board on one end of the top piece of timber, he can raise the board up tight to the ceiling by pressing down with his foot on the opposite end of the top piece – a simple but effective use of leverage. British Gypsum market a metal foot-operated lifter which fulfils the same function (reference G4 in their Gyproc tools brochure). Plasterboard to walls must be continuous, notwithstanding the fact that parts will be covered by baths, ducts, kitchen fittings etc.

When cutting boards around openings, vertical joints in line with reveals should be avoided. Generally speaking, plasterboard is a very tolerant material and, despite movement in timber-frame construction, cracking in plasterboard surfaces is most unusual. If, however, plasterboard is jointed in line with a reveal of an opening, the weakest part of the plasterboard surface is over the position where most movement is likely to occur.

Although not always specified in the UK, it is preferable to have plasterboard tacked by the double-nailing technique, using annular-ringed shank nails. Double nailing involves nailing with two nails approximately 25–30 mm apart at the specified centres, normally a maximum of 225 mm. This technique gives a first-class finish with little chance of nail-popping. This can occur with dry lining when the timber moves slightly and causes the nail head to protrude a little; creating an unsightly small bump on the plasterboard surface.

Great care should be taken in tacking staircase wells. It will be remembered that most shrinkage in a house occurs in the floor-thickness zone as timber shrinks mostly in its width, i.e. the floor joists shrink in depth. In Chapter 8, we saw how this is allowed for in respect of claddings. Internally, it only affects the staircase well. Horizontal joints in the plasterboard in the floor-joist zone of the staircase well should be left a little larger than elsewhere, thus requiring more filler. The theory behind this is that, when the joists shrink, the filler will be squeezed out and the filler is comparatively easy to rub down and redecorate. If boards are butted tightly together they tend to bulge out and become unsightly when the joists shrink. Some designers provide for a timber waist-band round the joist zone in staircase wells to cover the possible bulging of the plasterboard, the back of the waist-band being on the same plane as the face of the plasterboard.

Where more than one layer of plasterboard is specified, each layer must be fully nailed independently and the nails through the final layer should not be permitted to provide full support for all layers.

Tape-and-fill or jointing

Intermediate nail holes are normally filled by hand, even when the jointing is done by machine. The machine has an adaption for filling nail holes but operatives seldom use it.

Tapered-edge joints and angles are taped and filled either by the Ames machine or by hand. Although good results can be obtained

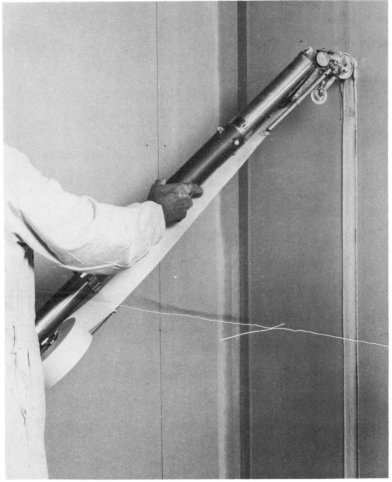

Fig. 9.1 Ames taping machine in operation.

by the skilled operator taping and filling by hand, the use of the Ames machine is certainly more extensively used, especially on the larger sites.

The process of mechanical jointing using the Ames machine consists of three main applications. Firstly, the machine is used to cover all joints and angles with a Gyproc joint tape (Ames) which is automatically applied with a limited amount of joint cement as the tape is unrolled off the machine and into position (see Fig. 9.1). The auto-taper attachment is used for this operation, with accessories added for internal angles. The tape used for external angles

Fig. 9.2 Finisher Box in operation.

is similar to that used for jointing but has two parallel rust-resistant metal strips bonded to its inner face to provide reinforcement to help resist light impact. It also assists the dry liner to produce a sharp and smooth angle. Where an external angle is in a very vulnerable position, likely to receive constant abrasion, a rigid angle bead should be used, of rust-resistant metal section to BS 2989: 1975. When this is used, it is imperative that it should be applied in one continuous length from floor to ceiling and well bedded in a suitable compound. After the tape application is dry, the first cement coat is applied, utilizing a box attachment 180 mm wide. This spreads the actual jointing compound to a width of 180 mm and is followed by the second and final cement coat, using a box attachment 250 mm wide, which is the width of the tapered edges of two abutting boards (see Fig. 9.2). When all these operations are dry, a light sanding by hand may be required to produce a perfect surface.

As the texture and porosity of the jointing compound is not always the same as that of the plasterboard surface, a fine slurry coat applied with a soft sponge over the whole surface to be decorated assists greatly in preventing the joints from 'grinning' through the first painting.

When an Ames taping machine is used, the operators keep the various parts of their machine in water, contained either in a plastic dustbin or 50-gallon drum. In cold weather and for reasons of security for their equipment, they tend to keep this equipment inside a house, where they also mix their jointing compound with water. All this can cause a lot of water spillage and mess. Site management should insist from the beginning of a job that, where these operations take place, the floor of the house is adequately protected.

It is worth mentioning here that British Gypsum provide free training courses in the use of the Ames machine and hand jointing.

Dimensions of plasterboards

Early in the history of modern timber-frame housing, before metrication was in use, careful taking-off of plasterboard requirements for each room was the normal practice. Dimensions of 4 ft by 8, 10, 12 and 15 (1.21 metres by 2.43, 3.04, 3.65 and 4.57) were available and the exercise was to use boards of maximum size with the minimum of waste, to avoid cutting, taping and filling. The North American practice was followed of tacking wall plasterboard horizontally and this proved very successful. Vertical joints were minimal, as few walls were over 15 ft (4.57 m) long without an opening. The one horizontal joint at mid-height becomes unde-tectable, even with strong side-lighting from a window at right angles.

Today, it is very difficult to persuade dry-lining operatives to accept horizontal boarding, they prefering to keep to 1200 × 2400 mm and 1200 × 2350 mm boards fixed vertically to walls. With the greater use of dry-lining techniques, the tape-and-fill operatives have become most efficient in their work and therefore, consider that the extra jointing created by vertical tacking is more economical than the extra work in fixing mid-height noggings, taking-off, ordering and loading-out involved in horizontal fixing to walls. It is strange that this is not the case in North America.

Ducts

Ducts are sometimes provided to conceal plumbing and s.v.ps. It is essential to finish these ducts in plasterboard to avoid the differ-ential movement and subsequent cracking bound to occur where the duct face meets the wall when the duct is finished in plywood. Plywood is often specified for this position because of the com-parative ease of providing removable access panels. However, access panels can also be provided in plasterboard with a little care-ful detailing, thus avoiding those unsightly gaps that occur where finished wall surface meets plywood duct at right angles.

Plasterboard is a strong, tolerant and fire-resistant material but must be handled, stored and fixed with respect and care.

10

Internal finishes

Finishes to internal walls and ceilings can be identical to those used in masonry construction. Indeed, in some instances, finishes are much easier to apply in timber-frame construction. 1200 × 2400 mm decorative panelling of sheet plywood is a good example, as it can be applied direct to the plasterboard, whereas, with masonry construction and wet plaster, battens would have to be applied and shimmed out to a true and level surface to receive the panelling.

The finishes to the plasterboard surfaces should be applied as soon as possible after the jointing has dried to prevent the plasterboard from soaking up any moisture vapour in the air.

Emulsion paint

Emulsion paint to dry-lined wall surfaces is probably most commonly used and gives a good serviceable finish. However, great care must be taken to ensure that the correct emulsion paint is used. Most paint manufacturers produce an emulsion paint which they market especially for first-time application to new plaster. They claim, quite correctly, that this emulsion paint, besides being cheaper, allows the wet plaster to dry out through the paint surface. With timber-frame housing and dry-wall construction, the problem of allowing the wet plaster to dry out through the paint does not apply and the first-time application emulsion is unnecessary. It should not be used if a first-class job is required because, although it is cheaper and covers well, it is not washable and is easily removed when occupiers try to remove dirty marks from walls.

Experience has shown that best results are achieved with emulsion paint when it is applied with a mohair roller. For most neutral colours, two-coat application will suffice. If dark colours or brilliant white are used, an additional coat may be required to obliterate completely the joints in the plasterboard.

Plastic ceiling finishes

Patent plastic ceiling finishes, such as Artex, are commonly used and are generally carried out by a specialist subcontractor. Consideration must be given to which operation is done first, the ceiling finish or the tape-and-fill to walls. Some experienced contractors prefer to get the ceilings completely finished before the tape-and-fill commences. Others prefer the opposite but, whichever is decided, and it is a matter of personal preference, two things must be remembered. The first is that whoever commences must be responsible for taping the ceiling to the wall joint and secondly, protection must be provided to the floors when the work is carried out to the ceilings.

Wallpaper

Wallpaper may be applied to dry-lined plasterboard, provided the plasterboard first receives a coat of sealer paint to facilitate ultimate removal of the wall paper without injuring the paper finish to the plasterboard surface. All paint manufacturers will advise on their recommended sealer for this work or Gyproc Drywall Top Coat by British Gypsum may be used.

Oil-bound paint

Oil-bound paint is sometimes specified for bathrooms and kitchens. A sealer coat is beneficial where dark colours or brilliant white is specified, whereas two coats of oil-bound paint in neutral colours will normally suffice without the sealer.

Painting generally

It should always be remembered that, with all forms of painting, the cost of the materials is a comparatively small proportion of the total cost of the work. It is, therefore, a false economy not to use a good-quality paint.

11

Ventilation

All timber incorporated in the construction of a house must be allowed to breathe, and kept dry and free from contact with moisture. The importance of a breather paper on the outside of the external panels has already been stressed but it was not so long ago that a timber-frame house was seen under construction where a designer had specified or, at least, the builder was using, bituminous roofing felt in lieu of breather paper. Roofing felt, being impervious, could cause disastrous effects when combined with the impervious vapour barrier on the inside of the external panels, as the timber between the two would be unable to breathe. It is to be hoped that building inspectors and designers are now becoming more experienced in timber-frame construction and will prevent this sort of thing, and that the case described above is a thing of the past.

Ventilation behind claddings has already been covered in Chapter 8 and general ventilation within the house to help prevent condensation on windows etc. is covered in Chapter 7.

Ventilation to roof space

We are, therefore, left with ventilation to the roof space. Although the underside of the roof space should be protected by the vapour barrier, a certain amount of leakage of moist warm air is sure to take place where pipes etc. perforate the vapour barrier and when the ceiling hatch is removed to gain access to the roof space. It is now mandatory under the Building Regulations (regulation (F5) 1338 of 1.4.82) to provide under-eaves ventilation at both front and back of a house, and this is provided in many ways by different designers. Probably the most popular way of providing it is by leaving a gap along one long edge of the eaves soffit, covered on the inside by chicken wire to prevent access to the roof space by birds. When the roof insulation is laid, although it must extend to the outside edge of the external panels to prevent a cold bridge, it must not extend further and so block the ventilation gap. On completion of the dwelling, it must be possible to see daylight on two sides of the house shining through into the darkened roof space. If it cannot be seen, it means that the insulation is blocking the ventilation gap and needs to be moved (see Fig. 11.1).

In addition to this requirement of the Building Regulations, it is recommended that the roof space be ventilated at high level by means of a ventilation ridge tile, which now appears to be ready available from most roof tiling manufacturers to suit most forms of roof tiling (see Figs 11.2–11.4).

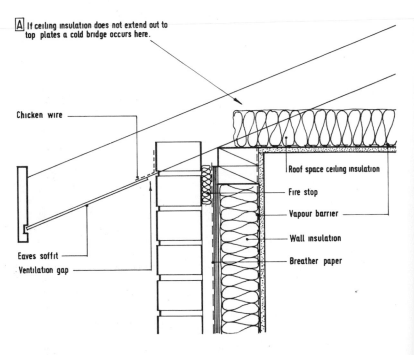

Fig. 11.1 Section of typical eaves detail showing ventilation gap and likely position of cold bridge if roof insulation does not extend past line of wall insulation.

78

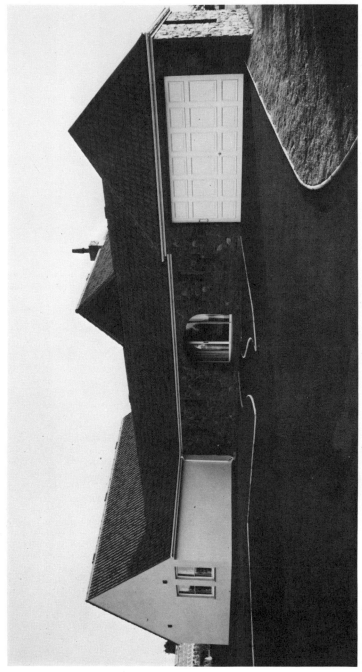

Figs. 11.2, 11.3 and 11.4 Three views of large FrameForm house in Guernsey, clearly showing ridge vent tiles to each roof.

Fig. 11.3

Fig. 11.4

12

Advantages of timber-frame housing in detail

Speed of erection

There can be no doubt that the well-organized contractor can consistently achieve a quicker construction cycle using timber frame than by using more conventional and traditional methods. The main reasons for this must include the quick erection of the prefabricated shell, enabling the roof to be completed within a few days of commencement and so providing the facility for men to work inside the house in the dry and comparatively warm conditions. The cladding being non-structural can proceed as weather conditions permit without seriously holding up the complete unit. The bricklayer does not become a critical trade in a critical path analysis. There is also the advantage to all trades working internally that all party walls and partitions are able to be walked through at will (as illustrated in Fig. 12.1) and all fixings, drillings and chases are into timber rather than masonry.

Higher degree of insulation more easily attainable

The various methods of insulating are covered in Chapter 7 and it will be remembered that by using brick cladding and 80 mm thick insulation between the 38×89 mm studs, a U value of 0.4 W/m^2 °C is achieved compared with the latest requirement of the Building Regulations of 0.6 W/m^2 °C through external walls. It is interesting to note here that traditional masonry construction, comprising brick outer skin, 50 mm cavity and lightweight concrete-block inner skin finished with wet plaster, produces a U value of 1.0 W/m^2 °C and, with full cavity insulation, it is improved to 0.45 W/m^2 °C.

Timber frame, being a highly-insulated lightweight structure, follows the principle of conserving within the external shell the

Fig. 12.1 Ground-floor components awaiting fixing of top plates. Note step and stagger condition at separating wall.

heat generated therein and also preventing the external cold and heat from the elements penetrating and influencing temperatures internally, that is to say, it keeps heat in, and keeps heat and cold out. With uninsulated solid masonry construction, before heat generated internally can be enjoyed, it has to warm up the structure. Once warmed, it will assist in keeping the internal areas warm. This, however, takes a considerable time to achieve. An easy experiment to prove this can be undertaken by merely putting your hand on an external wall inside a masonry-built house on a cold day when the inside temperature is acceptable. The wall will feel colder than the room. Do the same in identical circumstances in a timber-frame house and the difference in temperature between the room and the wall surface will be very much less.

Dry construction

It is estimated that between 1000 and 1500 gallons of water are used in the construction of a traditionally-built two-storey three-bedroom house. All this has to be dried out and this can be a long and costly operation. It can also cause a certain amount of discomfort to the occupiers when first taking occupation. With a timber-frame house, provided the screed is laid and dried before shell erection, the only water then used in the construction is that small amount used in the mixing of the jointing compound for the dry lining. Incidentally, in lieu of screed, some designers of timber-frame construction are successfully specifying sheet material, such as plywood or chipboard, laid on solid polystyrene sheets which are applied direct to the concrete slab between the sole plates. With this method, another wet trade disappears and, at the same time, improved thermal insulation is achieved at ground-floor level. The underside of the oversite slab has, of course, to be protected from rising damp by a damp-proof membrane in exactly the same way as for traditional construction.

Economy in construction

No-one can claim that timber-frame construction is generally cheaper than traditional construction. However, it is competitive with traditional and the builder who is keen on organization and methods is most likely to achieve larger financial gains in his construction costs. The quicker construction cycle produces smaller overheads and preliminaries, as well as earlier sales or rent receipts, and less incidence of interest charges on cost of land.

When competitive tenders have been obtained for large local-authority housing schemes where the tenderers have been given the option of tendering with traditional construction or timber frame, the results have not been always in favour of one or the other. When a contractor has been given the opportunity of pricing a contract both in masonry and timber-frame construction, which is the only fair comparison, i.e. same contractor, same time, same house types and same site, the timber-frame price has proved the cheaper about nine times out of ten. In fact, experienced timber-frame contractors have been known to offer a small percentage discount when submitting a tender for masonry houses if they are permitted to change the construction to timber frame.

The cost of materials in timber-frame construction is higher than the cost of materials used in its counterpart. However, the cost of site labour is lower and, while labour costs increase at a faster rate than costs of materials, as they have done now for some years, the advantage must inevitably swing more in favour of timber frame.

84

Less wastage of materials

With a high element of prefabrication, fully engineered and designed on a module to suit finishing materials, cutting and wastage of materials on site is kept to a minimum. The savings on waste materials is clearly evident to the experienced eye when seeing a well-run timber-frame housing site. It can also be seen in Fig. 1.2.

Higher standard of finish attainable

Because of the engineered design and prefabrication, the timber wall panels fit together accurately. Lengths of components are accurate which, in turn, create accurate and square rooms with right-angled corners. The plasterboard walls, being applied to C.L.S. studs which are accurately dimensioned and planed on four sides, achieve a true and level surface to receive finishing decoration. The absence of cracking in the plasterboard dry lining also gives a much smarter appearance. With traditional construction, wet plaster in any one room can be applied to three different materials, bricks, lightweight concrete blocks and concrete lintels. All these materials expand and contract under varying thermal conditions but, unfortunately, they do not expand and contract identically to each other. Cracks inevitably occur where two differing materials meet. We have all experienced lintel cracks, which are probably the most common example in traditional construction. In timber-frame construction, however, the dry lining is, without exception, fixed to timber and there is no differential movement to create the cracks.

Less maintenance

Although a timber-frame house will move and settle directly after occupation, the good designer will have allowed for the shrinkage in his details. Many years' experience has shown that the items on a list of defects found at the end of a six-months' defects liability period are minimal. Cracks in plasterwork are rarely encountered. Sometimes, doors on upper floors need easing but, apart from that, nothing is normally discovered that can be attributed to the fact that the house is timber-framed. Most items that appear on the defects list seem to concern the plumber, and specialist items, such as doors to kitchen fittings, which come adrift, floor tile which becomes loose, lock to front door which does not function properly and so on. One contractor who is well experienced in timber-frame construction claims that his maintenance costs on contract work with timber frame are about one quarter of his maintenance costs when building traditionally.

13

General hints

- Be prepared to accept that there are major differences from traditional construction in programming a timber-frame house and in the sequence of operations.
- Be extra careful over accuracy of ground-floor slab and fixing of sole plates.
- Keep treated timbers separate from untreated.
- See that all timber stored on site is adequately protected from the sun, as well as from the rain, but is allowed to breathe.
- When checking dimensions of timber, always combine with checking moisture content.
- When nailing 38 × 89 mm timber along its length through the 89 mm face, as for sole plates and top plates, never nail in a straight line down the middle. Always stagger the nails to help eliminate the chance of splitting.
- Drive all nails in at an angle, never at right angles to the face of the timber.
- Ensure that all nails and fastenings are rust-resistant.
- Use corrugated timber fasteners to join sole plates together before final fixing.
- Check levels of sole plates very accurately before final fixing.
- Carry out the screeding of the ground floor before commencing shell erection.
- Refer to labour employed on shell erection as timber frame erectors and not as carpenters. This may assist in satisfying the Safety Regulations.
- Give great thought to scaffolding. Bear in mind existing ground levels, openings, steps and staggers, type of cladding and type of roof. If a monopitch, loading-out can only be effected from the low side.

- Do not let shell erections proceed out-of-hand, ahead of following trades.
- Be careful not to overload floors with components, plywood or plasterboard during construction. Remember that floors are designed to carry 1.5 kN/m^2 (approximately 30 lb/ft^2).
- Give the supplier of the components and timber precise delivery requirements, including loading sequence on the transport.
- Treat roof trusses like sheets of plate glass.
- Release metal straps around packs of plywood if to be stored on site.
- Before completing ground-floor construction, ensure that staircase can be placed in position on completion.
- Before completing truss assembly, ensure that the water storage tank can be located on completion.
- Ensure that the whole of a flat-roof construction is adequately ventilated.
- Make sure all operatives understand the reason for the differing lengths of pre-cut noggings, i.e. those between studs are different from those between trusses or between floor joists.
- If not provided by the designer, prepare dimensioned sketches of rooms showing accurate location of noggings. This is essential for kitchens and bathrooms, and for radiator positions.
- Fixings for breather paper must coincide with fixings of sheathing plywood.
- The fixing of breather paper by staples through a strong plastic tape about 12 mm wide assists in keeping fixings in a straight line to coincide with internal studs and creates a much stronger fixing, because the breather paper is less likely to be pulled through the staple fixing.
- Ensure that the size and position of notching and drilling of joists does not exceed the limits set by the designer.
- Always mark on the surface of the plasterboard and floor deck the accurate position of water pipes they cover.
- Never run cold-water pipes adjacent to hot-water pipes without lagging.
- Overflow to cold-water storage tank to run at low level through roof space.

- Raise cold-water storage tank as high as possible in roof space if showers are to be provided on top floor.
- Provide bearers at right angles to joists under legs of bath and under hot-water cylinders sitting on the suspended floor.
- Never conceal waste and water pipes in stud walls.
- Ensure that printed matter on plastic s.v.ps, rainwater and waste pipes is turned out of sight when fixed.
- Never staple drops in electrical wiring to sides of studs within walls.
- Keep electrical wiring well clear of hot-water pipes.
- With a moisture meter, check that all structural timber is below 20 per cent moisture content before fixing insulation and vapour barrier.
- Ensure that no gaps occur in wall insulation.
- Ensure that vapour barrier provides as complete a seal as is possible.
- Keep wall insulation to the warm side; do not press back towards inner face of sheathing.
- Ventilate cavity behind all claddings.
- Use a gauge rod to ensure correct coursing of brickwork to reach sill and head heights of window and door openings.
- Plumb down from upper window reveals to ensure acceptable bonding of brickwork.
- Use two nails to every flexible brick tie, with the bottom one as near the bend as possible.
- Ensure that all cavity barriers and fire-stops are in position before cladding commences and remain so during the cladding operation.
- Provide expansion joints in brick cladding for lengths over 12 m.
- Pay particular attention to manufacturer's fixing instructions when using patent lathing to receive rendering.
- Stagger end joints in plasterboard ceilings.
- Stagger all joints where two layers of plasterboard are applied to one surface.
- Bottom edge of tacked plasterboard to walls should not be in contact with floor.
- Double-nailing technique using annular-ringed shank nails will give a first-class job with less chance of nail-popping.

- Determine at any early stage whether Artex ceiling finish is to be carried out before or after taping and filling of the walls. Whichever is done first must include the taping and filling of the ceiling to wall junction.
- No vertical joints in plasterboard to line with reveals to openings.
- Avoid timber-faced ducts abutting plasterboard walls. Face ducts with plasterboard wherever possible.
- Beware of non-washable emulsion paint.
- Mohair roller gives best results in application of emulsion paint.
- ✓ Plasterboard must be sealed before application of wall-paper.
- ✓ Insulation to roof space must extend to cover the external wall/ceiling junction but must not mask the under-eaves ventilation gap.

Appendix 1

Glossary of technical terms

Annular-ringed shank nail
Nail with a rough or deformed shank making it difficult to withdraw (see Fig. A.1).

Bay window
Window and floor which project beyond the main face of a building. When only the window frame projects, see projecting window.

Blind nailing
Nailing in such a way that the nailheads are not finally visible on the finished face.

Blockings
Pieces of timber placed at right angles between joists and of section the same size as the joists.

Bottom rail
Horizontal member of timber-frame wall panel that sits on sole plate or floor deck.

Breather paper
Material wrapped round external face of timber-frame shell to keep moisture out of timber frame from outside while allowing moisture under pressure to pass through it from inside.

Brick veneer
Half-brick thick cladding to timber-frame structure.

Building Regulations
The Building Regulations 1976 and subsequent amendments, a statutory instrument published by Her Majesty's Stationery Office.

Butt joint
Joint made by joining two members together end-to-end, without overlapping.

C.L.S.
Canadian Lumber Specification – stress-graded, planned four

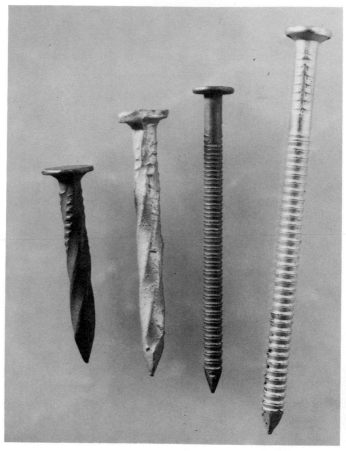

Fig. A.1 Square twisted nails on left, annular-ringed shank nails on right.

sides, arrises rounded and in standard-size sections. Some species of timber are always kiln-dried.

Cant strip
Wedge or triangular-shaped piece of timber as used round perimeter of flat roof where it meets wall to avoid dressing roof covering material into 90° angle. Also referred to as tilting fillet.

Cavity barrier
Complete obstruction placed in cavity to prevent spread of flame and smoke. To prevent cavity acting as flue.

Cavity-fill slab
> Material used to form cavity barrier.

Ceiling bracing
> Timber bracing battens on top side of ceiling chords of roof trusses.

Ceiling chord
> Bottom horizontal member of truss rafter to underside of which plasterboard is fixed to form ceiling to area directly below.

Cladding
> Non-structural material applied to outside of timber-frame shell to give decorative and weatherproof finish.

Cold bridge
> Leak in continuous insulation barrier caused by wall insulation which is cut short, leaving air space at top or bottom. Also caused by ceiling insulation which does not extend far enough to meet wall insulation (see Fig. 11.1).

Compartment floor
> Floor dividing units of accommodation within building.

Compartment wall
> Wall dividing units of accommodation within building.

Conditions
> Term used to signify differences between houses on layout. Steps in level, staggers on plan and different houses joined together in a terrace all produce 'conditions'.

Contraction
> Shrinkage of materials due to atmospheric conditions, e.g. timber contracts when excessive heat applied, causing lowering of moisture content.

Counterflashing
> Flashing applied above another to shed water over top of under-flashing and to allow some differential movement to joint protected, without damage to flashing.

Cripple stud
> Shortened stud used in wall panel to support lintel over opening. It fits between top of bottom rail and underside of lintel.

Dressed timber
> Timber that has been planed on all four sides. Wrought timber.

Dry lining
> Interior wall and ceiling finish achieved by nailing plasterboard to frame and filling nail holes and joints with filler compound.

Expansion
> Enlargement of materials due to atmospheric conditions, e.g. timber expands when moisture content increases due to exposure to wet conditions.

End grain
> Face of piece of timber exposed when fibres are cut transversely.

Fire-stops
> Fire-resistant material used in timber-frame construction to stop spread of flame from one building element to another.

Firring piece
> Piece of timber with one face tapered to provide sloping surface on top when laid flat on level surface, e.g. laid on top of joists to provide fall to flat roof.

Flitch beam or lintel
> Beam or lintel consisting of sandwich of two pieces of timber with steel core between them, all securely fastened together.

Floating floor
> Sound-deadening floor construction within each room resting on, but not secured to, structural joists. As used in constructing flats.

Floor deck
> Upper floor or platform on which upper-wall panels are erected.

Good one side
> Quality of plywood where knot holes are made good in finish of one side of each sheet.

Good two sides
> Quality of plywood where knot holes are made good to finish of both sides of each sheet.

Grading
> Classification of timber into established quality grades within the species.

Hanging scaffold
> Special scaffolding devised for timber-frame construction provided by hooking brackets over top of uppermost wall panels. These brackets receive walkways and guard rails. Brackets are dismantled externally after patent hooks are released internally.

Header joist
> Joist at right angles to series of joists where they terminate.

In stick
> Expression given to stacked timber which has battens at right

angles at intervals up stack to allow free circulation of air to all timbers within stack.

Joist clips
Metal fasteners used to secure ends of joists to top plates.

Joist hangers
Metal fasteners used to secure two joists together at right angles at same level.

KN/m²
Kilonewtons per square metre. Unit of weight-to-area ratio used in calculating loadings on floors, foundations etc. 1.5 kN/m² is the approximate equivalent of 30 lb/ft².

Ladder frames
Simple frames nailed to end truss, cantilevered over spandril panel to create roof overhang at gable ends.

Large-panel construction
Form of platform-frame construction where storey-height whole walls are made up as one panel, usually requiring lifting gear to hoist into position.

Lathing
Building element fastened to frame of a structure to provide base for rendered finish.

Moisture content
Amount of water contained in wood, usually expressed as percentage of weight of oven-dry wood.

Moisture meter
Small instrument, usually powered by torch batteries, used for measuring moisture content. Sensitive probes inserted into timber give reading on a gauge.

Nogging
Horizontal piece of timber fixed between vertical studs to provide solid fixing for fittings of all kinds.

Notching
Cutting out small sections of edge of timber, usually to allow passage of pipes across timber at right angles.

Panels
Units of wall construction – external wall panels, internal wall panels, window panels etc.

Plumb
Vertical. To make vertical.

Projecting window
Window only which projects beyond main face of building. If floor projects with window, it becomes a bay window.

Rafter bracing
> Timber bracing battens fixed to underside of roofing rafters of roof trusses.

Regularizing
> Defined in BS 4471 as process by means of which every piece of batch of constructional timber is sawn and/or machined to uniform width.

Reveal
> Visible part of each side of recess or opening in wall.

Roofing rafters
> Main angled timbers of roof truss to which roof covering is fixed.

Scabbing
> Expression used for fixing plate of metal or plywood to cover butt joints in floor joists.

Select sheathing
> Quality grade of plywood.

Separating wall
> Common wall separating two buildings. Known also as party wall

Sheathing
> Quality grade of plywood. Sheet material used on outside of external wall panels.

Shell
> Erected timber-frame structure complete, before following trades commence work.

Siding
> Cladding other than brick veneer or render.

Skew-nailing
> Nailing through side of one piece of timber at angle into face of another. See also toe-nailing and tosh-nailing.

Small-panel construction
> Platform-frame construction where storey-height walls are made up of panels that can be manhandled and nailed to each other on site without use of mechanical equipment.

Sole plates
> Timber members secured to foundations under all ground-floor wall panels.

Spandril panels
> Wall panels with top rails at angle of the roof pitch. When placed on top of top-floor wall panels at ends of house or terrace, they form gable end.

Square twisted nail
> Nail with square-section shank with twist in its length to prevent easy withdrawal (see Fig. A1).

Stitch nailing
> Nailing two pieces of timber together by driving nails at opposite angles through each of the two exposed sides so that they cross at right angles to each other.

Stick building
> Expression used when wall units are fabricated on site, i.e. panels are not prefabricated.

Stress grading
> Classification of timber into established quality grades within species.

Studs
> Full-height vertical members of all wall panels.

Suspended floor
> Any floor that does not have solid and complete bearing.

T. and G.
> Tongued and grooved.

Tacking
> Nailing plasterboard to timber frame.

Tape-and-fill
> Method of finishing tacked plasterboard by making good nail holes and covering joints with tape and filler compound.

Tapered edge plasterboards
> Plasterboards with wide bevelled edge along both long sides on face to facilitate tape-and-fill operation.

Template
> Pattern used as guide for setting out work.

Tilting fillet
> See cant strip.

Toe-nailing
> See skew-nailing.

Top plate
> Timber member of identical section to timber of panels, fixed along top of all wall panels.

Top rail
> Horizontal member at top of wall panel.

Tosh-nailing
> See skew-nailing.

Trimmer
> Joist alongside opening into which joists are framed.

Truss clips
>Galvanized metal fasteners nailed into top-floor top plates to receive and fix bearing positions of truss rafters.

Truss plates
>Galvanized metal plates that cover and hold together flush joints in timber prefabricated truss rafters. Held in position by either nails driven through pre-drilled holes in plates or projecting prongs on plates hydraulically pressed into the timber by various patented machines.

Truss rafters
>Prefabricated timber roof trusses, usually designed to span between external walls and comprising roofing rafters, ceiling rafters and intermediate supporting webs and struts, all in the same plane, joints in timbers covered and secured by truss plates.

Vapour barrier
>Material used to prevent passage of water vapour or moisture.

Volumetric
>Method of construction where sections of building are finished complete in factory and have only to be hoisted into position on site, on to prepared foundations, and then joined together.

$W/m^2 \, ^\circ C$
>Watts per square metre per degree centigrade, the unit used to measure heat loss through building elements (U value).

Appendix 2

Useful names and addresses

Organisation	Designation	Telephone number
British Gypsum Ltd, Ferguson House, 15 Marylebone Road, London, MW1 5JE.		01 406 1282
British Gypsum Product Training Centre, PO Box 6, Erith, Kent, DA8 1BQ.		
British Insurance Association, Aldermary House, Queen Street, London, EC4.	BIA	01 248 4477
British Standards Institution, 2 Park Street, London, W1A 2BS.	BSI	01 629 9000
British Wood Preserving Association, Premier House, 150 Southampton Row, London, WC1.	BWPA	01 837 8217
British Woodworking Federation, 82 New Cavendish Street, London, W1M 8AD.	BWF	01 580 5588
Building Research Establishment, Garston, Watford, Hertfordshire, WD2 7JR.	BRE	092 73 74040

Building Societies Association,
14 Park Street,
London, W1.   BSA   01 629 0515

Council of Forest Industries of British
   Columbia,
Tileman House,
131–133 Upper Richmond Road,
Putney,
London, SW15 2TR.   COFI   01 788 4446

Dry Lining and Partition Association,
15 South Street,
Lancing,
Sussex.   DLPA   090 63 5700

Fire Research Station,
Borehamwood,
Hertfordshire, WD6 2BL.   FRS   01 933 6177

House-Builders Federation,
82 New Cavendish Street,
London, W1M 8AD.   HBF   01 580 5588

International Truss Plate Association,
Twinaplate Ltd,
3 Milestone Industrial Estate,
Truro,
Cornwall, TR4 9LT.   ITPA   0872 79525

National House-Building Council,
Chiltern Avenue,
Amersham,
Buckinghamshire, HP6 5AP.   NHBC   024 03 4477

Princes Risborough Laboratory,
   (Formerly known as Forest Products
   Research Laboratory – FPRL)
Princes Risborough,
Aylesbury,
Buckinghamshire, HP17 9PX.   084 44 3101

Swedish Finnish Timber Council,
21 Carolgate,
Retford,
Nottinghamshire,
DN22 6BZ.   SFTC   0777 706615

Timber Research and Development
  Association,
Hughenden Valley,
High Wycombe,
Buckinghamshire, HP14 4ND.   TRADA   0240 24 3091

Timber Trades Federation,
Clareville House,
Whitcomb Street,
London, WC2H 7DL.   TTF   01 839 1891

Index

ROBERT
SCOTT